Praise for *A Theology o]*

Scholarly but accessible, clearly written but not simplistic, Chris Morgan's *A Theology of James* is an excellent example of biblical theology for the church.

—**Robert L. Plummer**, The Southern Baptist
Theological Seminary

Morgan deftly shows how James can—and does—interact in a clear, concise manner with the questions of the larger theological field. This book will be a much-needed addition to any pastor's library, a great guide for any Bible study group studying James, and a highly useful supplement to any college or seminary course on James.

—**Mariam Kamell**, Regent College

Dr. Morgan delivers a robust theological exposition of James with an eye to the needs of the contemporary church. He chooses key themes from the book and shows how they are developed, assisting the reader to see the pastoral heart of James in a new and more unified theological light. His insights issue a personal challenge to every reader.

—**John Massey**, Baptist Theological Seminary, Singapore,
International Mission Board (SBC)

Too often the theology of James is ignored or forgotten in the evangelical church. Chris Morgan reminds us in this wonderfully lucid, practical, and faithful rendition of James's theology that James's teaching is not only in accord with the gospel but fundamental to the gospel.

—**Thomas R. Schreiner**, The Southern Baptist Theological
Seminary

Morgan has produced a no-frills study rich with potential for injecting new fervor into churches tired of the status quo. Read it! Morgan not only explains to us James's teaching, he also commends to us the costly pattern of James's sold-out life.

—**Robert W. Yarbrough**, Covenant Theological Seminary

Praise for the Explorations in Biblical Theology series

Neither superficial nor highly technical, this new series of volumes on important Christian doctrines is projected to teach Reformed theology as it is most helpfully taught, with clear grounding in Scripture, mature understanding of theology, gracious interaction with others who disagree, and useful application to life. I expect that these volumes will strengthen the faith and biblical maturity of all who read them, and I am happy to recommend them highly.

—**Wayne Grudem**, Phoenix Seminary

There are many misconceptions today about systematic, biblical, and applicatory theology. One sometimes gets the impression that these are opposed to one another, and that the first two, at least, are so obscure that ordinary people should avoid them like the plague. The series Explorations in Biblical Theology seeks to correct these misunderstandings, to bring these disciplines together in a winsome, clear unity, edifying to non-specialists. The authors are first-rate, and they write to build up our faith by pointing us to Christ. That's what biblical and systematic theology at their best have always done, and the best application of Scripture has always shown us in practical ways how to draw on the rich blessings of Jesus' salvation. I hope that many will read these books and take them to heart.

—**John Frame**, Reformed Theological Seminary

The message of a God who loved us before he formed the earth, called us his own before we could respond to him, died for us while we were dead in our transgressions and sins, made us alive when we were incapable of serving him, unites us to himself so that we can be forever holy, and now loves us more than we love ourselves—sparked a Reformation of hope and joy that transformed the world of faith. Re-declaring that hope and reclaiming that joy is the ambition and delight of this series. Able and godly scholars trace the golden thread of grace that unites all Scripture to make the wonders of our God's redeeming love shine and win hearts anew. The writing is warm, winsome, and respectful of those who differ. The motives are clearly to reveal truth and expose error by glorifying the message and manner of the Savior.

—**Bryan Chapell**, Covenant Theological Seminary

The aim of these volumes is clear: as regards God's Word, rigor; as regards other scholars, respect; as regards current issues, relevance; as regards the Lord himself, reverence. Effective witness and ministry currently require more than extra effort and better methods: the call is heard from churches across the board for renewal in our grasp of Christian truth. Each author in this series contributes admirably to that urgent need.

—**Robert W. Yarbrough**, Trinity Evangelical Divinity School

This is a series that the church needs more than ever, as we forge fresh links between the world of biblical studies and our Reformed theology. The contributors remind us again that the Bible is a book about God and his purposes and encourages us to preach and teach the message of salvation which it contains. It will be an inspiration to many and will give us new insight into the faith once delivered to the saints.

—**Gerald Bray**, Beeson Divinity School

The church of Jesus Christ faces massive cultural challenges today. More and more people in the Western world are ignorant of or hostile to the Christian faith. The moral fabric of our society is unraveling, and as a result of postmodernism many are adopting a relativistic worldview. Some Christians have responded by trying to simplify and dumb down the gospel. Others have tried to catch the cultural mood of the day in order to gain more converts, but they have often been co-opted by the culture instead of transforming it for Christ. What we truly need is to dig down deep into biblical foundations, so that our theology is robustly biblical. Only a worldview that is informed by both biblical and systematic theology can withstand the intellectual challenges that face us today. The series Explorations in Biblical Theology is designed to meet this very need. I commend these volumes enthusiastically, for they explain what the Scriptures teach from the standpoint of biblical theology. What we desperately need to hear and learn today is the whole counsel of God. This series advances that very agenda for the edification of the church and to the glory of God.

—**Thomas R. Schreiner**, The Southern Baptist Theological Seminary

Explorations in Biblical Theology is a valuable new series of books on doctrinal themes that run through Scripture. The contributors are competent scholars who love to serve the church and have special expertise in the Bible and its theology. Following a thematic approach, each volume explores a distinctive doctrine as it is taught in Scripture, or else introduces the various doctrines taught in a particular book of the Bible. The result is a fresh and unique contribution to our understanding of the Bible's own theology.

—**Philip Ryken**, Wheaton College

Explorations in Biblical Theology is a gift to God's people. Biblical theology was never meant to be reserved for academics. When the verities of the Reformed faith are taken from the "ivy halls" of academia and placed in the hearts and minds of the covenant people of God, reformation and revival are the inevitable result. I believe God will use this series as a mighty tool for the Kingdom.

—**Steve Brown**, Reformed Theological Seminary

A Theology of James

Explorations in Biblical Theology

Robert A. Peterson, series editor

A Theology of James

Wisdom for God's People

Christopher W. Morgan

P U B L I S H I N G

P.O. BOX 817 • PHILLIPSBURG • NEW JERSEY 08865-0817

Printed in the United States of America

Library of Congress Cataloging-in-Publication Data

Morgan, Christopher W., 1971-
 A theology of James : wisdom for God's people / Christopher W. Morgan.
   p. cm. -- (Explorations in biblical theology)
 Includes bibliographical references and indexes.
 ISBN 978-1-59638-084-4 (pbk.)
 1. Bible. N.T. James--Theology. I. Title.
 BS2785.52.M67 2010
 227'.9106--dc22
                          2010039772

To my loving and joyful daughter Chelsey,
a precious gift from the Lord

Contents

Series Introduction

BELIEVERS TODAY need quality literature that attracts them to good theology and builds them up in their faith. Currently, readers may find several sets of lengthy—and rather technical—books on Reformed theology, as well as some that are helpful and semipopular. Explorations in Biblical Theology takes a more mid-range approach, seeking to offer readers the substantial content of the more lengthy books, on the one hand, while striving for the readability of the semipopular books, on the other.

The series includes two types of books: (1) some treating biblical themes and (2) others treating the theology of specific biblical books. The volumes dealing with biblical themes seek to cover the whole range of Christian theology, from the doctrine of God to last things. Representative early offerings in the series focus on the empowering of the Holy Spirit, justification, the presence of God, preservation and apostasy, and substitutionary atonement. Works dealing with the theology of specific biblical books include volumes on 1 and 2 Samuel, the Psalms, and Isaiah in the Old Testament, and Mark, Romans, and James in the New Testament.

Explorations in Biblical Theology is written for college seniors, seminarians, pastors, and thoughtful lay readers. These volumes are intended to be accessible and not obscured by excessive references to Hebrew, Greek, or theological jargon.

Each book seeks to be solidly Reformed in orientation, because the writers love the Reformed faith. The various theological themes and biblical books are treated from the perspective of biblical theology. Writers either trace doctrines through the Bible or open up the theology of the specific books they treat.

Writers desire not merely to dispense the Bible's good information, but also to apply that information to real needs today.

Explorations in Biblical Theology is committed to being warm and winsome, with a focus on applying God's truth to life. Authors aim to treat those with whom they disagree as they themselves would want to be treated. The motives for the rejection of error are not to fight, hurt, or wound, but to protect, help, and heal. The authors of this series will be godly, capable scholars with a commitment to Reformed theology and a burden to minister that theology clearly to God's people.

ROBERT A. PETERSON
Series Editor

Acknowledgments

GOD HAS MADE US for himself and to live in community with others. I am grateful for the community that God has placed in my life to shape me and my thinking. And while there are surely many errors in this book, I am convinced there are not nearly as many as there would be if it were not for these friends. There are too many to mention all of them, but I want to express gratitude to those who have made an impact on this project.

John Mahony, my professor, mentor, and friend, whose 1982 dissertation on James sparked my interest in the epistle, taught me to see it theologically, and inspired me to write this book.

Dale Ellenburg, my partner for *James: Wisdom for the Community*, whose exegetical observations and pastoral style have shaped some of what is here.

Colleagues and friends who read the manuscript and offered ways to strengthen the book: Dale Ellenburg, Mariam Kamell, John Mahony, John Massey, and Rob Plummer.

Friends and church leaders who read and offered helpful comments: Chris Compton, Kristen Harris, and Matt Leonard.

Many thanks also go to:

Malcolm Maclean and Christian Focus Publications for giving me permission to use portions of material from my aforementioned commentary on James.

My students in the Theology of James course at California Baptist University. Your hard work in translating, outlining, and reading James weekly, interacting with the major works on the epistle, working together in groups to study its themes and theology, and especially your desire to live out the message of James all make me feel honored to be your professor.

Dr. Ron Ellis, Dr. Jonathan Parker, Dr. Dan Wilson, the trustees, and the administration at CBU, for their consistent encouragement of my writing.

Librarian Barry Parker and student workers Kristen Harris, Matt Leonard, and Jonathan McCormick, for their diligence and assistance in the research process.

Robert Peterson, friend, partner, capable coeditor, and quality series editor, for his belief in this project and counsel throughout this process.

Finally, to Marvin Padgett and others at P&R, it is a pleasure to work with you. Your commitment to the historic teachings of the Christian faith, joyful spirit, and consistent support have been sources of much encouragement to me.

Introduction

NON-CHRISTIANS do not read the Bible; they read Christians. Because of this, the church's mission is inevitably tied to its example. Tim Keller points out that the Bible depicts "the extremely close connection between deed-ministry and word-ministry. The practical actions of Christians for people in need demonstrate the truth and power of the gospel. Acts of mercy and justice are visible to non-believers and can lead men to glorify God (Matt. 5:13–16)."[1] That the character and justice of the kingdom community are foundational to its witness was true of Israel and remains true for the church, as Christopher Wright explains: "The community God seeks for the sake of his mission is to be a community shaped by his own ethical character, with specific attention to righteousness and justice in a world filled with oppression and injustice. Only such a community can be a blessing to the nations."[2]

Indeed, many pastors and church leaders are inspired by knowing what the church can and should be. We invest our time, our prayers, our jobs—our very selves—in hopes of seeing the church become what God intends. The more we study and teach the Bible, the more we realize how important the church is. God elected it, Jesus bought it, and the Spirit indwells it. One day Jesus will present the church to himself as a perfectly beautiful bride. We also begin to notice that the church of the New Testament is imperfect, wedged historically in the eschatological already and not yet—and with power, personality, and cultural struggles. Yet in the New Testament we also see that the church is passionate about the gospel, serious about obeying Christ, diligent to take the

1. Tim Keller, "The Gospel and the Poor," *Themelios* 33, no. 3 (December 2008): 17.
2. Christopher J. H. Wright, *The Mission of God: Unlocking the Bible's Grand Narrative* (Downers Grove, IL: InterVarsity Press, 2006), 369.

gospel to all nations, generous in meeting the needs of the poor, and concerned to seek unity, even in the midst of some major cultural clashes between Jews and Gentiles.

However, the more we serve the Lord in our churches, the more we come to grips with another reality, this one a bit disheartening: most individual churches are not what they are supposed to be. These covenant communities do not exhibit as much passion for Christ, genuine love for others, servant spirit, or ministry to the hurting as we expect. Many churches exchange God's global purpose of making disciples of all nations for the task of maintaining the status quo. Much of their leadership, budgets, and programs are centered on themselves.

The irony is that we encounter these two truths at the very same time. The more we grow in our theology, the more value we place on the church. Yet the older we get and the more experience we have in serving churches, the more problems we see in the church. Biblically minded church leaders always have sensed— and until Jesus returns, always will sense—the tension between an ideal view of the church and a realistic view of churches. In fact, it is when pastors or church leaders stop feeling this tension that danger lurks. That is likely a sign of lowered standards, naïveté, or disillusionment. In many respects, the churches we serve are not what they are supposed to be, but this should not lead us to despair, but to service to the Lord who can strengthen them.

If we understand the biblical teaching regarding the already and the not yet, then this tension should not come as a surprise. It exists because the kingdom has already come in Christ, but has not yet been fully realized. The church, as the eschatological covenant community, is to bear the marks of the kingdom, yet will not do so perfectly until the grand finale of history, when the church is presented to Christ.

The epistle of James bears witness to this tension. This letter is written to real-life churches with real-life problems. Its message needs to be heard by churches today.

James, a key leader in the Jerusalem church, writes to help churches consisting of Jewish Christians who are struggling with oppression from without and strife from within. Some of them also slip easily into being religious without genuinely following Christ. Throughout his letter, James counters these problems and more as he offers wisdom for consistency in the covenant community, the church. And James addresses these challenges with a robust theology. While many think of the epistle of James as loaded with exhortations—and it is—it is much more than that. James offers pastoral instruction that is grounded in systematic theology. It is theology applied.

Like many epistles in the New Testament, the letter of James is comparable to an iceberg. The letter itself is like the visible portion that extends above the surface of the water. Yet what is underneath is much larger and shapes what is visible. The challenge of biblical theology is that we can only see what protrudes, but must also take into account the shaping mass that lies beneath. We cannot act as if what is visible is all that exists. Yet in our exploration of what is hidden, we must not distort what we do see. Hence, our goal is to examine the themes that lie above the surface, and then try to examine the underlying theology that shapes it.[3] Before we do, though, we should address some questions.

Why a Theology of James?

Many pastors and some church leaders are acquainted with both biblical exegesis and systematic theology. They have been taught how to read the Bible and how to teach or preach it in an expository manner. They have studied the major doctrines of the Christian faith, such as the doctrines of God, humanity, sin, Christ, salvation, the church, and last things. Many, however, have not drunk at the well of biblical theology. They have studied the particulars and the big picture, but they are usually not acquainted with what lies in between. An analogy might help. If we wanted to survey a large tract of land, we might do so from various points

3. I adapted this analogy from Richard B. Gaffin Jr., *Resurrection and Redemption: A Study in Paul's Soteriology*, 2nd ed. (Phillipsburg, NJ: Presbyterian and Reformed, 1987), 28.

of view. We might walk through it, drive through it, or fly over it in a helicopter. In a way, walking through it would be like biblical exegesis. Every piece of the terrain is observed. Flying over it is like systematic theology, as it orients us to the major contours of the land. Driving through it is comparable to biblical theology, as it covers the bulk of the terrain and yet gives a fairly broad perspective. All three approaches have their place.

While relying upon careful exegesis and being informed by systematic theology, this volume is a work in biblical theology and therefore seeks to connect the dots of the particular texts in the epistle of James and show its primary message. It also seeks to show the big picture of James, its specific themes, and how those themes point to the larger message. It seeks to demonstrate that while particular passages have important messages, biblical books also have larger, overarching messages that merit attention. Sometimes we get so focused on the specific truths of specific passages that we forget to read them in light of the overarching literary context. In contrast to our tendency, however, the epistle of James was likely written to be read to churches in its entirety, and thus was viewed primarily as a whole. A holistic look at James will enhance our understanding, teaching, and preaching.

I also feel the need for this book because James has received little attention theologically, although this is beginning to change. Much of the attention that James does receive is tied to the issue of justification (by faith alone or by faith and works). James's other themes and overall theology have much to offer and should not be neglected.

. In keeping with the purpose of the Explorations in Biblical Theology series, this volume does not address all of the scholarly debates concerning James, although those who are familiar with such debates will likely spot my views on many of the issues. Instead, I will set forth the primary themes and theology of James, so that the big picture of its message can be better seen. I will also assess how James's teaching is related to, and informed by, other biblical writers. And upon that foundation I intend to sketch out the overall theology of James.

What Is "a Theology of James"?

The title of this book indicates that James has a coherent theology and is by nature theological. Something of a theology of James can be uncovered through a careful reading of this epistle. James is not too obscure to make this theological quest impossible or foolish. James's theology serves as a presupposition to his letter and is to some extent traceable in it. His exhortations are based upon his theology, which seems to be rooted in the Old Testament, Judaism, and the teachings of Jesus. James has a theology, and we can to some extent discover it.

However, a full-blown theology of James cannot be uncovered (it is hard enough to construct a theology of Paul). After all, the epistle has only five short chapters and was written to address specific needs; it is not a textbook of systematic theology. James's theology is present to a greater extent than most scholars have recognized and serves as the underpinnings of his letter, but it is not as carefully constructed as Paul's. So I do not claim to produce here *"the* theology of James." Nevertheless, by looking carefully at the epistle, we can make strides toward understanding James's theology. Or, to return to our iceberg imagery, we can understand what we see above the surface, and we can detect some things that lie beneath the surface, but we cannot know as much as we would like about what lies beneath.

How Do We Examine the Theology of James?

We begin in chapter 1, "James in Context," by examining the historical and literary context of James. This chapter provides the background information necessary to interpret James. Reading without knowing the context is like listening to one part of someone else's conversation—we may only understand a portion of it. "James in Context" addresses James and his ministry, the churches and their problems, and the epistle and its characteristics.

In chapter 2, we examine "Influences on James's Thought." No one writes as an island unto himself. James was no different. He was significantly influenced by the Old Testament law, prophets, and wisdom literature. Even more, James displays an incredible dependence upon the teachings of Jesus. This can be seen in every section of the letter. The more we see how James is rooted in the teachings of the Old Testament and Jesus, the more we can understand his theology.

The next step is to consider the particular teachings of James in their immediate literary context. This, however, is the task of a biblical commentary and not this volume. I have not skipped this crucial step, however, since I recently coauthored (with Dale Ellenburg) just such a commentary: *James: Wisdom for the Community.*

Building upon that exegetical foundation, we strive to ascertain the major themes of James. "James's Pastoral Burden: Wisdom for Consistency in the Community" (chapter 3) summarizes the central, integrative concern of James, which shapes the other themes. Those themes are then examined in chapters 4 through 9: wisdom, consistency, suffering, the poor, words, and God's word and law.

With that background, we are then able to examine the well-known issue concerning James and Paul. James 2:14–26 often raises questions about its compatibility with Paul's theology of justification by faith apart from the works of the law. In "James and Paul" (chapter 10), we examine those questions.

Then we sketch out James's larger theology in chapter 11. We see James's theological contributions concerning God, humanity, sin, Christ, salvation, the Christian life, the church, and last things. In chapter 12, we see how James's theology functions in his letter.

Finally, James's message for first-century churches merits the attention of our own twenty-first–century churches. Accordingly, the final chapter proposes that James's God-centered theology, vision of the church, holistic approach to salvation and mission, and integrative method of theology serve as helpful correctives to, and models for, both traditional and missional churches.

James in Context

WHO WROTE the epistle of James? When, to whom, and why was it written? What literary style, form, and structure does it have? As we find the answers to these questions, we will discover something pivotal for interpreting the letter: behind the epistle of James lies the story of a minister urging churches to be more consistent in their Christian walk.

James and His Ministry

In his greeting, the author identifies himself as "James, a servant of God and of the Lord Jesus Christ, to the twelve tribes in the Dispersion: Greetings" (1:1). Three views on the identity of the author stand out.

James, the Brother of Jesus?

The author names himself "James," but does not elaborate. This lack of elaboration probably means that he had no need to do so, as he was known by his readers and was probably recognized widely in the church. The traditional view is that James, the brother of Jesus, is the author. He was the most prominent leader bearing this name in the early church.[1]

1.Douglas J. Moo, *James*, Tyndale New Testament Commentaries (Grand Rapids: Eerdmans, 1985), 19–20 (hereafter abbreviated as Moo, *James*, TNTC). Because of the virgin

1

What do we know about this James? In their lists of Jesus' brothers, both Matthew and Mark list James first ("James and Joseph and Simon and Judas," Matt. 13:55; Mark 6:3), probably as the oldest of the four. This would make him the second oldest of the brothers, after Jesus of course. And though James and the other brothers occasionally accompanied Jesus during his ministry, both in Galilee (John 2:12) and in Jerusalem (John 7:1–10), they did not believe in Jesus during that time (John 7:5; cf. Mark 3:13–21).

Sometime after the resurrection, however, Jesus' physical brothers believed and became his spiritual brothers. John Stott notes, "It is remarkable, therefore, that during the ten days which elapsed between the ascension and Pentecost, the brothers of the Lord are specifically mentioned by Luke as finding their place in the believing, praying company of expectant Christians (Acts 1:14)."[2] What happened? Paul sheds some light on this in his account of Jesus' resurrection appearances, stating

> . . . that Christ died for our sins in accordance with the Scriptures, that he was buried, that he was raised on the third day in accordance with the Scriptures, and that he appeared to Cephas, then to the twelve. Then he appeared to more than five hundred brothers at one time, most of whom are still alive, though some have fallen asleep. Then he appeared to *James*, then to all the apostles. Last of all, as to one untimely born, he appeared also to me. (1 Cor. 15:3–8)

James witnessed not only Jesus' resurrection, but probably his ascension as well (Acts 1:1–14). James was present in the upper room after the ascension, when Matthias was selected to replace Judas as one of the twelve apostles (Acts 1:12–26). And when the day of Pentecost arrived, James was there, beholding the work of the Holy Spirit and the inauguration of a "new era

---

birth, some refer to James as the half-brother of Jesus. For the sake of style, however, I will refer to him simply as James, the brother of Jesus.

2. John R. W. Stott, *Men with a Message: An Introduction to the New Testament and Its Writers*, rev. Stephen Motyer (Grand Rapids: Eerdmans, 1994), 120.

in which the eschatological life of the future invades the present evil age in a proleptic manner."[3] Further, James probably heard Peter's sermon at Pentecost and saw three thousand people come to believe in Jesus, repent of their sins, be baptized, and become a part of the new covenant community.

So it is likely that James witnessed Jesus' resurrection, became a believer, then also witnessed Jesus' ascension, the reconstitution of the Twelve, the outpouring of the Holy Spirit at Pentecost, and the formation of the church! It is no wonder that James became an important leader in the early church, especially among Jewish Christians. His prominence is clear from the story of Peter being rescued from imprisonment by Herod (who had just killed James, the brother of John). Note Peter's request, "Tell these things to James and to the brothers" (Acts 12:17). That James is the one to be made aware of this indicates that he was "a major figure in the Jerusalem church."[4]

We also learn of James's stature in the early church through Paul's epistle to the Galatians. Paul refers to James as an "apostle" (Gal. 1:18–19), and, along with Peter and John, a "pillar" (Gal. 2:9). Paul viewed these three as key leaders in the Jerusalem church and met with them to discuss the gospel and his missionary strategy. Paul later described the accord: "And when James and Cephas and John, who seemed to be pillars, perceived the grace that was given to me, they gave the right hand of fellowship to Barnabas and me, that we should go to the Gentiles and they to the circumcised. Only, they asked us to remember the poor, the very thing I was eager to do" (Gal. 2:9–10).[5] James, Peter, and John backed Paul and his understanding of justification by faith apart from circumcision, which defended him against some influential Jewish opponents. This unity in the gospel would be displayed

3. Sinclair B. Ferguson, *The Holy Spirit*, Contours of Christian Theology (Downers Grove, IL: InterVarsity Press, 1996), 57.
4. Darrell L. Bock, *Acts*, Baker Exegetical New Testament Commentary (Grand Rapids: Baker, 2007), 430.
5. Note how this theme is also prominent in the epistle of James. For more on the poor in the Jerusalem church, see Acts 4:32–35; 6:1–4; Rom. 15:25–33; 1 Cor. 16:1–4; 2 Cor. 8–9.

as Gentile Christians shared their resources with the poor in the Jerusalem church.

Paul later discovered that Peter, himself an apostle and a pillar, had stopped eating with the Gentiles after "certain men came from James" (Gal. 2:12). As in his previous denial of Christ before the crucifixion, Peter yielded to peer pressure. This disappointed Paul, given Peter's previous vision of Cornelius (Acts 10–11) and recently stated convictions about the full inclusion of the Gentiles in the church. Who were these "certain men" who "came from James" and negatively influenced Peter? They were not necessarily the "false brothers" of Galatians 2:1–6, who pushed for the circumcision of Titus, and thus the necessity of circumcision for full inclusion in the church. Timothy George states:

> Nor should we assume that James had engineered their [the men from James's] action as a ploy to win Peter back to a more hard-line position on Gentile fellowship. Obviously these visitors felt some attachment to James, respected his leadership of the church in Jerusalem, and perhaps even carried letters of recommendation from him (cf. 2 Cor. 3:1–3). Later at the Jerusalem Council, James, writing to the believers in Antioch, referred to certain persons who "went out from us without our authorization and disturbed you, troubling your minds by what they said" (Acts 15:24).[6]

George is right. There is no need to see these men as representing James, but only coming from Jerusalem and potentially distorting the ideas of James.[7] The biblical accounts display an overall unity between Paul and James, even as they faced radically different contexts and concerns.

Acts 15 is also significant in this respect, recounting the important role that James played in the early church. The theo-

---

6. Timothy George, *Galatians*, New American Commentary (Nashville: Broadman and Holman, 1994), 175; cf. 128–202.

7. This is interesting and ironic. As we will see later, some interpret James 2:14–26 as a response to a misunderstanding or distortion of Paul's teachings (sometimes called "Paulinism"), and Paul here in Galatians may be correcting a distortion of James's teachings (shall we call this "Jacobeanism"?).

logical and missiological concerns raised by Paul in Galatians 1 had been brewing and finally came to a head. Some Jewish leaders maintained that circumcision was necessary for salvation. Paul and Barnabas opposed those leaders and their views and "were appointed to go up to Jerusalem to the apostles and the elders" and address this question (15:2). At this so-called "Jerusalem Council," Paul and Barnabas declared how God had genuinely converted Gentiles. Some Jewish believers opposed Paul and Barnabas and their conclusions. After much debate among the apostles and elders, Peter delivered a powerful case for God's acceptance of the Gentiles, Paul and Barnabas testified again, and then James spoke:

> Brothers, listen to me. Simeon has related how God first visited the Gentiles, to take from them a people for his name. . . . Therefore my judgment is that we should not trouble those of the Gentiles who turn to God, but should write to them to abstain from the things polluted by idols, and from sexual immorality, and from what has been strangled, and from blood. For from ancient generations Moses has had in every city those who proclaim him, for he is read every Sabbath in the synagogues. (Acts 15:13–21)

In this speech, James spoke authoritatively ("listen to me") and showed his support of Peter, even highlighting his Jewish name, Simeon. James explained that God had visited the Gentiles and called them as his people. James pointed to Amos 9:11–12 to remind the assembly how God had promised a future restoration, which included gathering a remnant of his people together. That remnant included the Gentiles. This had all happened because the Messiah has come. The arrival of the Holy Spirit confirmed that the new age had dawned and that the Gentiles were included, just as the prophets had previously announced. The present people of God stood in continuity with Israel, but extended also to the Gentiles. What appeared to be new was "really an old promise."[8] I. H. Marshall explains:

8. Bock, *Acts*, 505. Paul later echoed this emphasis (cf. Rom. 15:7–13).

The point would seem to be that God is doing something new in raising up the church; it is an event of the last days, and therefore the old rules of the Jewish religion no longer apply: God is making a people out of the nations and nothing in the text suggests they should become Jews in order to become God's people. So there are no entrance "conditions" to be imposed upon them.[9]

James asserted that the Gentiles must not be burdened with Jewish regulations, but out of respect and cultural sensitivity should refrain from certain matters (15:20).[10] Following James's speech, the apostles and elders commissioned a letter to the Gentile believers, stating essentially what James had just asserted.

James's leadership role among the Jewish Christians was significant. He seemed to serve as the chair at the Jerusalem Council, his conclusions regarding the controversy won the day, and his insightful speech solidified the council's decision.

Acts 21:17–26 portrays another episode involving Paul and James. Paul and Luke arrived in Jerusalem and went to see James and the elders. Paul told them stories of what God had done among the Gentiles. Upon hearing the stories, James and the elders glorified God (21:20). But they also informed Paul that many Jewish Christians had been hearing false reports of Paul's teaching and ministry. The word on the street was that Paul had been undermining the law by telling Jewish Christians neither to circumcise their children nor to follow traditional customs. So James and the elders encouraged Paul to go into the temple and publicly perform the rites of purification, which would help silence the rumors and demonstrate his commitment to the law. At their request, Paul did so.

Acts 21 also sheds light on James, Paul, and their relationship. For example, it shows how people misinterpreted Paul's teaching

9. I. H. Marshall, *The Acts of the Apostles*, Tyndale New Testament Commentary (Downers Grove, IL: InterVarsity Press, 1992), 253; see also Christopher J. H. Wright, *The Mission of God: Unlocking the Bible's Grand Narrative* (Downers Grove, IL: InterVarsity Press, 2006), 348, 501, 518–19.

10. Paul later reflected the same concerns (cf. Rom. 14:1–15:7). In German, such limitations for the purpose of cultural sensitivity are known as *Jakobsklausen*, or "James clauses" (Bock, *Acts*, 507).

concerning the law. Paul preached that justification was by faith in Christ, not by the works of the law. But many Jewish Christians construed Paul to be teaching that the law was unimportant. Paul taught that circumcision was not necessary for salvation, but he was rumored to be teaching Jewish Christians not to circumcise their children.

Acts 21 also shows the ministry context in Jerusalem (21:20–21). Paul was preaching the gospel to Gentiles and declaring that they could be saved apart from the Jewish works of the law. James was preaching the gospel to Jews and needed to show how Christianity is consistent with, the extension of, and the climax of the law and its teachings. These contextual differences are quite significant to our interpretation of Paul and James. Paul held a high view of the law, but stressed that salvation comes in union with Christ and his saving work, is initiated by and brought about by God's grace, and is received by faith—not through circumcision, eating the right food, keeping the Sabbath, or performing good deeds. Neither being Jewish nor keeping the law brought about salvation. God did. And because of this, Gentiles were to be received as equal members of the people of God.

Thankfully, Paul and his theology have received so much attention that his context and emphasis are now often understood (though there is dispute regarding the details). The same cannot be said for James, however, as his writing and contexts are often overlooked. James wrote to help Jewish Christians understand how the coming of the Messiah inaugurated the new age, and how this should shape their understanding of salvation, the law, the Gentiles, the covenant, and the people of God. James had the monumental task of showing how Christianity is the extension and the fulfillment of Judaism, and how this was articulated by the prophets of old. He led the Jerusalem church at a time when the city was tense with rising Jewish nationalism, political unrest, and Roman occupation. Jewish Christians were likely taking flack from the Romans on one side and Jewish loyalists on the other. James and the Jerusalem church did not share the traditional, anti-Gentile spirit. Instead, they were caught in the middle, trying to relate to and evangelize Jews and yet support and defend the Gentile mission. That is why James made the purification request of Paul, and that is why Paul, himself passionate about the salvation of the Jews (cf. Rom. 1:16–17; 9:1–6; 10:1), humbled himself and complied. Both James and Paul desired to show that Paul was a "loyal Jew and that outreach to the Gentiles is not anti-Jewish."[11]

Contrary to scholars like F. C. Baur, the New Testament portrays Paul and James as preserving remarkable harmony, given their different needs and contexts. There were tensions from time to time, but too much has been made of this. Neither Paul nor Luke was afraid to point out the messiness of leadership and the friction that often results when strong personalities are involved. Yet the biblical accounts reveal that both James and Paul guarded the gospel of grace, and they did it in unity.

Further, both James and Paul employed wise cross-cultural strategies. Because most Christians are Gentiles today, we tend to read their accounts and assume that Paul was the one sacrificing for the good of the whole. He definitely was, and much can be learned from that. But we should also realize that James was paying a high price for defending the gospel, Paul, and the Gentile mission. James and the Jerusalem church had to live in Jerusalem after Paul moved on to the next city. They had to address the misunderstandings multiplied by gossip and riots. Their credibility with local Jewish loyalists kept getting weaker, which inevitably made their evangelism of the Jews more difficult. It also became harder to keep Jewish Christians from being confused by the clamor. Marshall puts it well: "We probably underestimate what a colossal step it was for dyed-in-the-wool Jewish legalists to adopt a new way of thinking. Moreover, it is possible that nationalist pressure was increasing in Judea, and that Christians were having to tread carefully to avoid being thought of as disloyal to their Jewish heritage."[12]

11. Bock, Acts, 643.
12. Marshall, Acts, 249.

Beyond these biblical accounts, the information on James is sketchy and based on various reports by early historians.[13] They mention that he was the first "bishop" of Jerusalem, was nick-named "James the Just" because of his devotion to prayer and faithfulness to the law, and was martyred in Jerusalem in AD 62. Josephus recounts that James was highly regarded by the people of Jerusalem, but feared and hated by the priestly aristocracy that ruled the city. The high priest, Ananius, had James brought before the Sanhedrin, tried, and stoned.[14]

Why is this James, the brother of Jesus, likely to have been the author of this letter? First, as we will see below, he is the only viable James mentioned in the New Testament. Second, the testimony of the ancient church supports this.[15] Third, the Greek contains striking similarities to the speech and letter by James recorded in Acts 15:13–21, 23–29. Moo maintains:

> The epistolary "greeting" (*chairein*) occurs in James 1:1 and Acts 15:23, but only one other time in the New Testament; the use of name (*onoma*) as the subject of the passive verb "call" (*kaleo*) is peculiar, yet occurs both in James 2:7 and Acts 15:17; the appeal "listen, my brothers" is found both in James 2:5 and Acts 15:13; and there are other slight similarities. These parallels are certainly not numerous enough to provide proof of common origin, yet they are suggestive when taken in conjunction with the first two points.[16]

Fourth, the Jewish flavor of the epistle is consistent with what we know about James, the brother of Jesus. The Old Testament allusions, the proverbial nature of the wisdom sections, the prophetic style of admonitions, the reference to the synagogue, and

13. See Matti Myllykoski, "James the Just in History and Tradition: Perspectives of Past and Present Scholarship (Part I)," *Currents in Biblical Research* 5, no. 1 (2006): 73–122; idem, "James the Just in History and Tradition: Perspectives of Past and Present Scholarship (Part II)," *Currents in Biblical Research* 6, no. 1 (2007): 11–98.

14. John R. W. Stott, *The Message of Acts: The Spirit, the Church and the World*, Bible Speaks Today (Downers Grove, IL: InterVarsity Press, 1990), 121–23; cf. D. H. Little, "The Death of James the Brother of Jesus" (PhD diss., Rice University, 1971).

15. Moo, *James*, TNTC, 22.

16. Ibid., 22.

the strong monotheistic emphasis all resonate with the biblical accounts of this James. Fifth, the teachings of Jesus, especially in the Sermon on the Mount, are strikingly reflected in this letter. This too would be appropriate from a brother of Jesus who was with him during certain parts of his earthly ministry. Sixth, James's leadership position in the early Jewish Christian church would have made it natural for him to address authoritatively the needs and concerns of "the twelve tribes in the Dispersion" (1:1). Finally, central themes in the epistle like the poor and suffering/ persecution are characteristic of the other biblical portraits of the concerns of James, the brother of Jesus.

Another James or an Unknown Christian Leader?

Some scholars have suggested that another James or an unknown Christian leader in the early church was the author of the epistle. Three arguments stand out.

First, it is hard for some to believe that the brother of Jesus would not have mentioned, or at least alluded to, that relationship in the letter. Such a relationship would have bolstered his authority with the churches.

Second, the language and cultural background of the epistle are sometimes seen as inconsistent with the author being the brother of Jesus. Ralph Martin comments:

> Aside from the issue of direct authorship, the most secure conclusion is that this document—whether in epistolary form or not—betrays a debt to the literary conventions and idioms of Hellenistic Judaism. It may have some connection with James in Jerusalem; but its final author, whether as redactor or amanuensis, was well versed in the bilingual vocabulary and writing techniques of the Roman provinces.[17]

Though not personally holding to this view, Moo states the argument clearly: "James is written in idiomatic Hellenistic Greek,

17. Ralph P. Martin, *James*, Word Biblical Commentary (Waco, TX: Word, 1988), lxx.

with some literary flourishes (cf. the incomplete hexameter in 1:17), and occasionally employs language derived from Greek philosophy and religion (e.g., 'the cycle of nature' in 3:6)."[18]

Third, some suggest that the theological use of law in the epistle varies from the heavy commitment to the law found in James, the brother of Jesus. The epistle depicts the law as "the law of liberty" (1:25; 2:12) and "the royal law" (2:8) and focuses on the moral law, with no mention of the ceremonial law. This, it is argued, does not fit together well with Jesus' brother's emphasis on the law, including his stress on its ceremonial and ritual aspects.[19]

What then are the alternative suggestions? A few argue that the epistle was written pseudonymously (written under the false name of James by an individual or a community in the tradition of James for the purpose of gaining authority and/or extending his teachings). Peter Davids dismantles that hypothesis: "Against the theory of pseudonymous authorship stands the simplicity of the greeting, the lack of exalted titles ('brother of the Lord,' 'elder in Jerusalem,' or 'apostle of Christ'); for a pseudonymous author would most likely identify his James better and would stress his authority."[20] Terry Wilder also makes a strong case that "the extant documentary evidence indicates that the early church did not accept pseudonymity. When discovered, it was soundly rejected."[21]

Others propose that the author could have been another James mentioned in the New Testament, or one who went unmentioned, since James (*Iakobos*) was a common name. The New

18. Moo, *James*, TNTC, 24–25.
19. Martin, *James*, lxx–lxxi. For an assessment of these arguments, see Moo, *James*, TNTC, 23–28.
20. Peter H. Davids, *The Epistle of James*, New International Greek Testament Commentary (Grand Rapids: Eerdmans, 1982), 9.
21. Terry L. Wilder, J. Daryl Charles, and Kendell Easley, *Faithful to the End: An Introduction to Hebrews through Revelation* (Nashville: Broadman and Holman, 2007), 59; cf. Terry L. Wilder, "Pseudonymity and the New Testament," in *Interpreting the New Testament*, ed. David Alan Black and David S. Dockery (Nashville: Broadman and Holman, 2001), 296–335. James D. G. Dunn disagrees. See his "Pseudepigraphy" in *Dictionary of the Later New Testament and Its Developments*, ed. Ralph P. Martin and Peter H. Davids (Downers Grove, IL: InterVarsity Press, 1997), 977–84.

Testament records at least three distinct men named James, besides Jesus' brother.

First, there was James, the son of Zebedee, who became a follower of Christ near the outset of Christ's ministry (Mark 1:19). One of the twelve disciples, this James was often mentioned with his brother John, and was a member of Jesus' inner circle (with John and Peter). He was beheaded at the command of Herod Agrippa I in AD 44 (Acts 12:1–2).

A second James was the son of Alphaeus. He too was one of the twelve disciples and receives mention only in Mark 3:18 (unless he is James the "lesser," or "younger," referenced in Mark 15:40; cf. Matt. 27:56).[22]

There was a third James, who was the father of Judas. This Judas, not the infamous Judas Iscariot (John 14:22), is listed as one of the twelve disciples (Luke 6:16; cf. Acts 1:13; called "Thaddaeus" in Matt. 10:3 and Mark 3:18).

These alternatives, however, are problematic. James, the brother of John, was martyred in AD 44, and it is highly unlikely that this letter was written before then. Most scholars also reject the latter two candidates because they would have needed to identify themselves better if "the twelve tribes in the Dispersion" were expected to submit to their authority. Is it possible that another James penned this epistle? Yes. Is that the strongest position? No. The traditional view makes much more sense of the evidence.

Teaching from James, the Brother of Jesus, and Later Redaction?

The third major approach to the authorship of James is the two-stage development view, which holds that James, Jesus' brother, is responsible for the teachings of the letter, but that the letter itself may have been composed by another person or a Christian community. This view exists in various forms. Scholars who defend a two-stage development view include Ralph Martin and Peter Davids.

22. Moo, *James*, TNTC, 19.

Martin suggests that the letter originated with the teaching of James, the brother of Jesus, who was martyred in approximately AD 62. Then, after the Jewish War of AD 66–70, the community of which James had been a part left Palestine and settled in Syria. There they continued to follow the teachings of James, refined them, and created a letter, the epistle we know as James, to address a pressing pastoral problem.[23]

Davids maintains that some of the material in James points to an early date, between AD 40 and the Jerusalem Council (approximately AD 50). He supports this from the author's self-designation, the strong Jewish influence, the use of a preliterary tradition of the words of Jesus, and the lack of a developed Christology. Yet Davids also finds evidence of a later date from the Greek idiom, the contextual factors that would occasion such strong teaching on poverty and wealth, and some similarities to the Apostolic Fathers. He theorizes that the teachings of James, the brother of Jesus, stand behind the source material, but that he received assistance in the editing of this material, either during his lifetime or perhaps after his death, as the church spread beyond Jerusalem and began to use Greek more exclusively.[24]

The two-stage development view is much stronger than the "another James" view. It is possible, but unnecessary. It is helpful, however, in that it underscores that James, the brother of Jesus, stands behind this epistle and its teachings.

The Churches and Their Problems

Date

If James, the brother of Jesus, is the author of this letter, then it was written before AD 62, the date of James's martyrdom. The lack of references to issues surrounding the Jerusalem Council (e.g., law, Gentiles, kosher food, etc.) may point to a date prior to the Jerusalem Council (approximately AD 50). The

23. Martin, *James*, lxvii–lxxvii.
24. Davids, *James*, 22.

references to severe poverty would especially make sense if the letter of James was written after the famine in Jerusalem in AD 46 (Acts 11:28). This would also coincide with initial versions of the social, political, and religious upheavals that culminated in the Jewish war of rebellion in AD 66–70.[25] This early date also seems consistent with the strong emphasis on the traditions of Jesus' teaching, with the church depicted as "synagogue," and the letter's dependence on Jewish sources.[26] Thus, a date between AD 46 and 49 is tentatively proposed. If this is correct, James might be the earliest written of the books to be included in the New Testament.

The Churches/Recipients

Although a detailed explanation of the historical situation and audience cannot be found in James, the letter does provide some information about the audience, sometimes explicitly, but most often implicitly. One characteristic is clear: the recipients were primarily, if not exclusively, Jewish Christians. This seems clear from James 1:1 as well as regular references to Jewish institutions and beliefs. These Christians also met in a synagogue (2:2) with elders (5:14). Their God is immutably holy (1:13–15), one (2:19), and the unique judge and lawgiver (4:12). James refers to Abraham, Rahab, and Elijah. He expects his readers to understand the Old Testament image of the marriage relationship as representing the covenant between God and his people (4:4).

Where did these Jewish Christians live? James 1:1 addresses "the twelve tribes in the Dispersion." I. H. Marshall observes that while this is a Christian letter to Christians, "the writer here takes up the tradition of Jewish leaders writing to Jewish people living in exile from their homeland and exposed to the difficulties and trials of this situation."[27] Most scholars interpret this literally, as refer-

---

25. Douglas J. Moo, *The Letter of James*, Pillar New Testament Commentary (Grand Rapids: Eerdmans, 2000), 25–27 (hereafter abbreviated as Moo, *James*, PNTC).

26. Ibid., 26.

27. I. H. Marshall, *New Testament Theology: Many Witnesses, One Gospel* (Downers Grove, IL: InterVarsity Press, 2004), 628.

ring to Jewish Christians who were scattered among the nations. Others point out that this phrase was used in intertestamental Judaism as a reference to the true people of God in the last days (cf. 1 Peter 1:1). It is possible that these Jewish Christians were located in Palestine and given this label as an encouragement to stand firm through trials because of the eschatological hope they possessed. But more likely they were Jewish Christians literally scattered among the nations.[28]

From where would a letter to scattered or exiled Jewish Christians likely come? Richard Bauckham aptly answers: "A letter to the Diaspora must come from Jerusalem. A Christian letter to the Diaspora could come from no one more appropriately than from James."[29] He adds that along with Peter and Paul, "James was one of the three most influential leaders in the first generation of the Christian movement."[30] This is in part because the Jerusalem church functioned for many as the mother church, as central and authoritative. With their heritage of acknowledging Jerusalem and its temple, Jewish Christians may have thought of the Jerusalem church as more lofty than we might think of it. Moreover, the Jerusalem church not only played a part in the conversion of many of the scattered Jewish Christians, but also sent out many missionaries and would have received many who came back to Jerusalem for the festivals.

From the depiction in 1:1, the letter from James in Jerusalem appears to be an encyclical, that is, one sent to a number of churches. Bauckham makes a compelling case for this, and critiques James Adamson's comparison of James to 1 Corinthians because it overstates the occasional nature of James. If it is an encyclical, Bauckham argues, everything stated in the letter is intentionally vague and hypothetical. While Bauckham is right

28. For more on the twelve tribes in the Diaspora, see Robert W. Wall, "James, Letter of," in *Dictionary of the Later New Testament and Its Developments*, ed. Martin and Davids, 548–51; cf. P. R. Trebilco, "Diaspora Judaism," in *Dictionary of the Later New Testament and Its Developments*, ed. Martin and Davids, 287–300.

29. Richard Bauckham, *James: Wisdom of James, Disciple of Jesus the Sage* (London: Routledge, 1999), 16.

30. Ibid.

to warn against too meticulous a reconstruction of an occasion, he goes too far when he asserts, "It is unlikely to have been occasioned by any specific exigencies."[31]

I believe that James writes in a particular context to address specific needs of the Diaspora churches. Marshall captures the tension: "We thus have the paradox that the writer appears to be writing to a very broad audience, the Christians scattered among the nations, and yet seems to have a very specific congregation or congregations in view."[32] I suggest that James writes his letter because he knows these churches and wants to address their real needs. Even an encyclical is written out of a context, to a context, and for a purpose.

The recipients were part of local congregations (2:2) with teachers (3:1) and elders (5:14). These Jewish Christians were experiencing significant trials (1:2–4) and serious oppression (2:6; 5:1–11). Some in their ranks were claiming they had faith, but they had little concern for personal holiness (1:22–25; 4:4) and failed to assist the poor or the marginalized (1:26–27; 2:1–13, 14–26). The congregations included others who wanted to be viewed as teachers, but were unworthy (3:1–12). Such people were quarrelsome, creating factions rather than peace (3:13–4:10). While these are common problems facing churches, James's consistent emphasis on a few themes, coupled with his impassioned arguments, suggests that these were issues already encountered by these churches. Further, James's attitude and message hardly lead anyone to conclude that these churches were healthy. A hypothetical encyclical would not be as negative as this epistle, or would include more positives along the way (would not some of the churches be healthy?).

What can be made of the socio-economic level of the recipients? Since the letter is probably an encyclical, this would vary to some extent, though the cultural norms would often prevail from church to church. James 1:9–11 refers to "the lowly brother" who will ultimately be exalted. This suggests recipients who were low on the socio-economic scale. Yet 2:1–13 evaluates how these

31. Ibid., 25–28.
32. Marshall, *New Testament Theology*, 629.

recipients have treated the rich who attend their assembly in comparison to those who come and are poor with "shabby clothing." Some in the church gave preferential treatment to the rich and dishonored the poor, which was particularly absurd since most of them were poor (2:6). The recipients were generally able to meet the needs of those fellow church members who were poorly clothed and in need of daily food (2:14–26). From this it appears that there was a certain minority in the churches that had major financial needs, but also a larger group that was not severely poor. The majority at least had decent clothes and daily food, and even enough resources to help their fellow believers.

More information about the recipients comes from 4:13: "Come now, you who say, 'Today or tomorrow we will go into such and such a town and spend a year there and trade and make a profit.'" Such an exhortation makes little sense unless there were at least some in the congregations who were merchants. James also addresses the rich in 1:9–11 and 5:1–6, and from this some have concluded that the congregations must have included wealthy landowners. That is highly improbable since James depicts such people suffering future punishment in hell. Instead, James uses a rhetorical style reminiscent of some of the Old Testament prophets and condemns the rich outside the fellowship.

This reconstruction of the audience suggests that there are four distinct groups referred to in this epistle: (1) the poor (the majority in this believing community), (2) the severely poor (those without decent clothes and often in need of daily food), (3) the merchants (those tempted to be overconfident in their plans), and (4) the wealthy landowners (those exploiting the poor).[33] The congregations were primarily composed of the first three groups, with the majority being in the first category.

33. More than one hundred years before the writing of James, the Roman general Pompey conquered Judean territory and left many Jewish peasants without land. Later the extreme taxation by Herod the Great drove more small farmers out of business. The result was that in the first century many peasants worked as tenants on large estates while others became day laborers, hoping to find good work and often finding it only around harvesttime. Resentment against aristocratic owners was significant and often deserved. See Craig Keener, *The IVP Bible Background Commentary* (Downers Grove, IL: InterVarsity Press, 1993), 688.

In sum, it seems best to conclude that James, the brother of Jesus, wrote from Jerusalem around AD 46–49 to churches he knew, in order to address their needs. These churches were composed primarily of Jewish Christians who were working poor. These churches faced challenges from the outside (oppression from the rich) and turmoil on the inside (lack of love for the extreme poor, political power plays for leadership roles, disunity, slander against one another, etc.).

The Epistle and Its Characteristics

Language and Style

Most scholars agree that James was written in a fairly elevated form of literary Koine Greek. Davids remarks:

> This can be concluded from a host of observations: the use of subordination (with conjunctions) and participial constructions rather than coordination, the careful control of word order (e.g., the placing of the stressed object before the verb, the separation of correlated sentence elements for emphasis as in 1:2; 3:3, 8; 5:10), the relative lack of barbarisms and anacolutha [i.e., an abrupt change in grammatical structure], the use of the gnomic aorist (1:11, 24), and choice of vocabulary. . . . All of these point to a developed literary ability.[34]

James is also characterized by an unusual vocabulary. One estimate is that James contains 63 *hapax legomena* (words found only once in the New Testament). Thirteen of these 63 appear in James for the first time in Greek, while 45 are found in the Septuagint, a pre-Christian Greek translation of the Old Testament.[35]

James also uses many Semitisms. Some examples of Hebrew influence on his style include the use of the passive to avoid stating God's name (1:5; 5:15) and parallelism (1:9, 11, 13; 4:8–9;

34. Davids, *James*, 58.
35. Ibid., 58–59.

5:4). Further evidence of Jewish background is provided by the fact that the believers gather in the synagogue (2:2), acknowledge Abraham as their "father" (2:21), and know God as "the Lord of hosts" (5:4, the only time this name is used in the New Testament). At a bare minimum, the thought-world of James incorporates Jewish concepts and ideas.

In addition, James employs many analogies. He writes of waves driven and tossed by the sea (1:6), withering plants (1:10–11), looking into a mirror (1:23), a dead body (2:26), bridling of a horse (3:3), a rudder turning a ship (3:4), a forest fire (3:5–6), taming wild beasts (3:7), the absurd fountain of fresh and bitter water (3:11), the absurd vine of grapes and figs (3:12), the vanishing vapor (4:14), clothes eaten by moths (5:2), and farmers waiting for the harvest (5:7).[36]

One striking literary feature is James's use of hook words or phrases that link together clauses and sentences.[37] For example, patience (1:3–4), maturity (1:4–5), asking (1:5–6), testing/temptation (1:12–14), lust (1:14–15), and anger (1:19–20) are used in this way.

Form

As is evident from James 1:1, the genre of James is *epistle*. It opens with an address that mentions its author, its recipients, and the general occasion.

Although James is primarily an epistle, other literary forms can be detected. For example, James is also *paraenesis* (exhortation). Paraenesis is "a genre of ancient moral literature characterized by various collections of moral sayings and essays, loosely held together by common themes and linking catchwords but without literary rhyme, theological reason or specific spatial location."[38] Its dominant mood is imperative, and the primary exhortation is to live virtuously. It often points to

36. Kurt A. Richardson, *James*, New American Commentary (Nashville: Broadman and Holman, 1997), 24.
37. This is called duadiplosis or paronomasia.
38. Wall, "James," 551.

moral truth that all should accept and heroic examples that all should imitate.[39]

James in some ways also bears the imprints of oral composition. The material may originally have been a collection of *sermons* by James later put into writing as a letter under his authority and oversight.[40] Various elements in James not only demonstrate the author's literary skill, but also his accomplished rhetorical style and oral composition. This is seen in James's overall flow and rhythm, along with the particular usage of paronomasia (1:1–2), parechesis (1:24), alliteration (1:2), rhyme (1:6), and similarity in word sounds (3:17). There are also several indications of an oral style in James: relatively short sentence structure, frequent use of the imperative (49 times in 108 verses), forms of direct address (17 occurrences of the vocative, primarily "brothers"), vivid examples, personification (1:15, 23), simile (1:6, 10–11; 5:7), rhetorical questions (2:6–7, 14, 17; 4:1, 5), and negative terms (2:20; 4:4, 8). Davids concludes, "All of these examples together show that despite its careful literary crafting, the letter partakes of the characteristics of oral rather than written discourse."[41]

Structure

The epistle's structure, or lack thereof, often takes center stage in academic discussions. Some find little or no literary strategy and structure. Reformer Martin Luther supposed that James threw things together chaotically.[42] Martin Dibelius proposed that James has minimal structure and is primarily paraenesis, a collection of exhortations loosely strung together.[43] Others, however, note structure and progression. Following the trajectory of

39. See Matt. A. Jackson-McCabe, "A Letter to the Twelve Tribes in the Diaspora: Wisdom and 'Apocalyptic' Eschatology in the Letter of James," *Society of Biblical Literature Seminar Papers* 35 (1996): 504–17.

40. C. L. Church, "A Forschungsgeschichte on the Literary Character of the Epistle of James" (PhD diss., The Southern Baptist Theological Seminary, 1990), 255–61.

41. Davids, *James*, 58.

42. Timothy George, "'A Right Strawy Epistle': Reformation Perspectives on James," *The Southern Baptist Journal of Theology* 4, no. 3 (Fall 2000): 20–31.

43. Martin Dibelius, *A Commentary on the Epistle of James*, rev. Heinrich Greeven, Hermeneia Commentary (Philadelphia: Fortress, 1976), 1–11.

Fred Francis, Davids argues that James is a "carefully constructed work."[44] Finally, some like Moo proffer that James displays key motifs that are replayed and interwoven throughout the letter, but that his structure is not as neat as some suggest.[45]

Many of the best proposals suggest that James has a thematic introduction in some part of chapter 1, and then develops those themes throughout. Robert Wall, for instance, proposes that 1:1–21 functions as a thematic introduction, centered around 1:19, which is developed in 1:22–2:26 as the wisdom of "quick to hear," in 3:1–18 as the wisdom of "slow to speak," in 4:1–5:6 as the wisdom of "slow to anger," with 5:7–20 being concluding exhortations.[46]

Davids suggests that James begins with an opening statement (1:2–27), which includes the primary themes unpacked in the remainder of the epistle. Davids sees 2:1–26 as developing the theme of 1:9–11 and 1:22–25: the excellence of poverty and generosity; 3:1–4:12 as developing the theme of 1:5–8 and 1:19–21: the demand for pure speech; 4:13–5:6 as developing the theme of 1:2–4 and 1:12–18: testing through wealth. Davids agrees with Wall that 5:7–20 constitutes a closing statement.[47]

This approach to structure seems promising, though I tend to think that using 1:26–27 as the governing text in the opening statement makes the most sense out of James. It highlights themes of consistency, genuine faith, words, mercy to the fragile, and keeping oneself from the world.

Moo organizes an outline around one key theme: spiritual wholeness. He puts forward the following structure: address and greeting (1:1); pursuit of spiritual wholeness: trials (1:2–18); evidence of wholeness: obedience to the word (1:19–2:26); community dimension of wholeness: pure speech and peace, part 1 (3:1–4:3); summons to wholeness (4:4–10); community dimension

44. Davids, *James*, 25; cf. Fred. O. Francis, "The Form and Function of the Opening and Closing Paragraphs of James and 1 John," *Zeitschrift für die neutestamentliche Wissenschaft* 61 (1970): 110–26.
45. Moo, *James*, PNTC, 45.
46. Wall, "James, Letter of," 557–59.
47. Davids, *James*, 22–29.

of wholeness: pure speech and peace, part 2 (4:11–12); worldview of wholeness: understanding time and eternity (4:13–5:11); concluding exhortations (5:12–20).[48]

The best recent proposal for James's structure comes from Mark Taylor and George Guthrie:[49]

1:1	The Opening of the Letter
1:2–27	Double Introduction: Living by Righteous Wisdom
1:2–11	Handling Trials with Righteous Wisdom
1:2–4	The Spiritual Benefit of Trials
1:5–8	The Need for Righteous Wisdom
1:9–11	Wise Attitudes for the Rich and Poor
1:12	*Overlapping Transition: Blessings for Those Who Persevere under Trial*
1:13–27	The Perils of Self-Deception

┌1:13–15   Temptation's True Nature
└1:16–19a ┐ Do Not Be Deceived: God Gives the Word
┌1:19b–21 ┘ Righteous Living through the Word
└1:22–25   Do Not Be Deceived: Be Doers of the Word

1:26–27	*Transition: Self-Deception Regarding Speaking and Acting*
2:1–5:6	Living the "Law of Liberty"
A 2:1–11	Body Opening: Violating the Royal Law through Wrong Speaking and Acting Inappropriately toward the Poor
B 2:12–13	**So Speak and So Act as One Being Judged by the Law of Liberty**

48. Moo, *James*, PNTC, vi–vii, 43–46.
49. Mark E. Taylor and George H. Guthrie, "The Structure of James," *Catholic Biblical Quarterly* 68 (2006): 681–705; cf. Mark E. Taylor, "Recent Scholarship on the Structure of James," *Currents in Biblical Research* 3 (2004): 86–115; idem, *A Text-linguistic Investigation into the Discourse Structure of James* (London: T & T Clark, 2006); Luke L. Cheung, *The Genre, Composition, and Hermeneutics of James* (Waynesboro, GA: Paternoster, 2003).

Influences on
James's Thought

IN ORDER TO INTERPRET the themes and theology of James, we need to examine what shapes James's thought. His teachings and thought-world are rooted in and reflect both the Old Testament (the Law, the Prophets, and the Wisdom Literature) and the teachings of Jesus.[1]

Old Testament Law

James's teachings and thought-world are deeply rooted in the Old Testament, including the Law. In fact, three of James's six Old Testament quotations (all in James 2) are taken from the Law. Echoing Jesus, James 2:8 quotes from Leviticus 19:18, "You shall love your neighbor as yourself." James refers to this as "the royal law according to the Scripture" (2:8). Observing a fascinating relationship between James and Leviticus 19, Luke Johnson notes, "What is more striking

1. Because of the purposes of this series, we will not address theories about James and sources, Q, the Synoptic Gospels, Peter, or nonbiblical Jewish literature that James at times seems to echo. Because there are only two unambiguous references to the Old Testament historical literature (Rahab in Joshua 6:25 and Elijah in 1 Kings 17–18), it will not receive treatment. Potential cases of intertextuality will be noted on occasion. Cf. John W. Mahony, "The Origin of Jacobean Thought" (PhD diss., Mid-America Baptist Theological Seminary, 1982), 170–257. Note also that James and 1 Peter draw on three of the same Old Testament passages: Isaiah 40:6–8 in James 1:10–11 and 1 Peter 1:24; Proverbs 10:12 in James 5:20 and 1 Peter 4:8; Proverbs 3:34 in James 4:6 and 1 Peter 5:5.

is the way that he places this in the framework of partiality in judging, showing a clear allusion to Leviticus 19:15."[2] James 5:4 refers to Leviticus 19:13, and James 4:11, 5:9, 5:12, and 5:20 may be thematic allusions to Leviticus 19:12–18. Shared themes include the poor, the command not to steal, God's name, just payment of daily wages to workers, protection of the vulnerable, impartiality toward the poor and the rich, the prohibition of slandering others in the covenant community, and the centrality of love for one's neighbor.

James 2:11 quotes from the Ten Commandments in Exodus 20:13–14 (cf. Deut. 5:17–18).[3] James lists the commandments in the same order as that of the Septuagint (rather than the Hebrew Old Testament): "Do not commit adultery," followed by "Do not murder." James quotes Exodus 20:13–14 and speaks to several issues related to Exodus 20–23. Common themes include God as jealous, covenant love, God's name, the commandment against murder, the commandment against adultery, orphans and widows, the poor, slander, courts of justice, and justice for the poor versus killing the innocent.

James 2:23 quotes from Genesis 15:6, "Abraham believed God, and it was counted to him as righteousness." This is a key verse in both James's and Paul's understanding of faith and will be addressed in the chapter "James and Paul."

That James's teachings are rooted in the Law is clear, not only from his quotations, but also from his allusions, echoes, references, and convictions. For example, Mariam Kamell argues that Deuteronomy 10:12–22 serves as a helpful backdrop to understanding James. She finds several topics in common: God's election of his people, impartiality, justice for orphans and widows, provision of food and clothing to strangers, love for God leading to loving others, and God shaping community ethics.[4] James's

2. Luke Timothy Johnson, "The Use of Leviticus 19 in the Letter of James," *Journal of Biblical Literature* 101, no. 3 (1982): 393.

3. See Richard Longenecker, *Biblical Exegesis in the Apostolic Period* (Grand Rapids: Eerdmans, 1975), 200.

4. Mariam Kamell, "The Economics of Humility: The Rich and the Humble in James," in *Economic Dimensions of Early Christianity*, ed. Bruce Longenecker and Kelly Leibengood (Grand Rapids: Eerdmans, 2009), 157–75.

command to hear and obey the word (1:22–25) also reflects the Torah, especially Deuteronomy 6–7. James's emphasis on the unity of God (2:19) reflects the Shema, and his assertion that humans are created in the image of God, and are therefore significant and worthy of respect, comes from Genesis 1:26–28. James's explanation of faith and works is reminiscent of covenant faithfulness and has roots in the narratives of Abraham and Isaac in Genesis 15–22.[5] James's convictions regarding God as Lawgiver and Judge echo the Old Testament law. In sum, the teachings of James are firmly anchored in the Old Testament, including the Law, which he considers trustworthy, unified, and authoritative for Christians.

Old Testament Prophets

James resembles the Old Testament prophets in tone, style, and content. A. M. Hunter called James "the Amos of the new covenant."[6] The prophetic resemblance is particularly clear in such passages as James 1:22–27; 4:1–10; 5:1–6. In James 1:22–27, this prophetic approach is seen in his command that the people of God hear the word and do it. This mirrors prophetic teachings like Ezekiel 33:32. James's assertion of God's demand for personal holiness in conjunction with the promotion of love and justice for widows and orphans as reflective of true religion stands in continuity with Isaiah 1:10–20.

In James 4:1–10, the prophetic tone, style, and themes appear in James's rebuke of worldliness (4:4), his reference to sin as spiritual adultery and as a violation of our covenant relationship with God (4:4; cf. Hosea; Isa. 54:5–6; 57:3; Jer. 3:20; Ezek. 16),[7] his firm reminders of God's jealousy for his people (4:5) and for pure worship (4:5; cf. Zech. 8:2), and his denunciation of the proud (4:6–7; cf. Isa. 61:1; Zeph. 3:11–12). This approach is also evident in James's exhortation to "draw near,"

---

5. James 2:21 refers to the Septuagint (usually abbreviated LXX) by using the word *anenenkas* ("offered," the same term used in Genesis 22:2 LXX).

6. A. M. Hunter, *Introducing the New Testament* (Philadelphia: Westminster, 1948), 98.

7. Jesus also refers to "a wicked and adulterous generation" (Matt. 16:4; cf. 12:39).

or return, to God (4:8; cf. Zech. 1:3; Hos. 12:6), his commands
to wash and clean one's hands and heart (4:8; cf. Isa. 1:10–20;
66:17), and his imagery of repentance as grieving, mourning,
and wailing over sin (4:9; cf. Isa. 15:2; Jer. 4:13; Hos. 10:5; Joel
1:9–10; 2:12; Mic. 2:4).[8]

Nowhere is the epistle more influenced by the Old Testament prophets than in James 5:1–6. Like Amos, James bluntly
rebukes the proud and wealthy landowners who exploit and
oppress the poor (Amos 8:4–6). James draws a picture of their
impending doom. They will suffer affliction, their possessions
will be ruined and witness against them, and their flesh will be
consumed as by fire (e.g., Amos 1:12, 14; 5:6; 7:4; Isa. 30:27–28;
51:8; Jer. 5:14; Ezek. 15:7). The storehouses of their wealth will
become storehouses of coming wrath (Amos 3:10–11; 6:10–15;
Mic. 2:7). The rich will be judged like animals headed to the
slaughterhouse (Isa. 34:2–6; Jer. 12:3; 25:34–50). Further, God
himself takes note of the wages they withhold from the poor
day laborers (e.g., Jer. 22:13). Using the terminology of Isaiah,
James describes the warrior God and his power to judge—the
Lord of hosts (Isa. 1:9; 2:12; 5:9; 6:3). Even James's imperative
"listen" (2:5) and address "come now" (4:13) are in keeping with
the prophetic style and tone (e.g., Isa. 51:4, 7).

Other strands of material in James also point to roots in the
Old Testament prophetic tradition. For example, James's consideration of himself as a servant stands in continuity with both the
Old Testament prophets and the teachings of Jesus. John Mahony
observes: "The servant-concept was a popular self-designation
among the Old Testament prophets, e.g., Amos 3:7, Daniel 9:6,
10; Zechariah 1:6; Isaiah 34:23; 42:19; and Malachi 4:6."[9]

James's teaching frequently alludes to or mirrors Old Testament prophetic material. His use of a wave as a picture of the
instability of the wicked (1:6) resembles Isaiah 57:20, "But the
wicked are like the tossing sea." James's use of the grass to illus-
trate the temporary nature of life (1:10–11) parallels Isaiah 40:6–8,

8. Mahony, "Origin of Jacobean Thought," 173–83.
9. Ibid., 175.

and his reference to the scorching heat of the east wind (1:11) is reminiscent of several prophets (Hos. 13:15; Jer. 18:17; Jonah 4:8; Ezek. 17:10). James's emphasis on death as the consequence of sin stands in continuity with Ezekiel 18:4, and his concept of the people of God as a sort of "firstfruits" (1:18) is similar to Jeremiah 2:3. His use of the prophets as examples of those who persevere also illustrates this.

In sum, while James is not a prophetic work per se (it is an epistle), it is significantly influenced by the tone, style, and themes of the Old Testament prophets. This is particularly pronounced in its calls for hearing and doing, genuine religion, protection of the oppressed, heartfelt repentance, and judgment on the rich exploiters.

Old Testament Wisdom Literature

The letter of James also reflects the Old Testament wisdom literature. This is seen as James describes how rich people "drag" the poor into court (2:6; cf. Job 20:15 LXX), the "withering" of the rich (1:10–11; cf. Job 15:30 LXX), and the call to perseverance (chapters 1 and 5; cf. Job 15:31 LXX). James also uses analogies that show his dependence on the Old Testament wisdom traditions. He compares the brevity of life with the fading flower (1:11; cf. Prov. 27:1; Eccl. 12:6; Job 13:28) and references the movement of the heavenly bodies (1:16–18; cf. Job 38:33 LXX).[10]

Other examples abound. The truth that "God opposes the proud, but gives grace to the humble" in James 4:6 is a quotation from Proverbs 3:34 LXX. James's analogy of the tongue as a fire (3:6) resembles the teachings of Proverbs 16:27 and 26:21, and the tongue as a poison is similar to Psalm 140:36. James's linking of wisdom and peace (3:13–18) is in keeping with Proverbs 3:17. James's call for mourning rather than

---

10. Ralph P. Martin, *James*, Word Biblical Commentary (Waco, TX: Word, 1988), lxxxvii–xc.

laughing (4:9) is similar to Ecclesiastes 7:2–7. James's casti-
gation of the all-too-frequent presumptuousness (which he
equates with boasting) in human planning (4:13–17) applies
Proverbs 27:1, "Do not boast about tomorrow, for you do not
know what a day may bring." The temporary nature of life
is depicted in the same text as a vapor or mist (4:14), which
is similar to Job 7:7, Psalm 102:3, and the overall tenor of
Ecclesiastes. Plus, James's overall idea in 4:13–17—that human
plans are contingent and God's will is sovereign—resembles
Proverbs 19:21, "Many are the plans in the mind of a man, but
it is the purpose of the LORD that will stand."[11] James's use of
Job as a model of endurance also shows dependence on the
Old Testament wisdom tradition (5:10–11). James similarly
links wisdom with themes such as the gift of God, words, suffering, peace, the transitory nature of life, prayer, and faith.
Further, James's teaching about God's law reflects Psalm 19,
and so do his interrelated themes of life, wisdom, joy, purity,
cleanness, righteousness, and reward.

In addition to having deep roots in the Old Testament
wisdom tradition, James has a primary concern to teach about
wisdom and its practical results. James applies the truths about
God and his ways to such daily issues as trials, temptations,
words, wealth, obedience, planning, and the brevity of life.[12]
In doing so, the author stresses that we find wisdom solely in
God and that our response to daily challenges must be consistent with God's person and ways. James's opposition to being
double-minded and his call for wholeness and integrity underscore his practical approach to wisdom. Living in a unified and
consistent manner is wisdom rightly applied. James teaches
in the Israelite-Jewish tradition and consciously reflects the
wisdom traditions.[13]

11. Mahony, "Origin of Jacobean Thought," 173–83.
12. For more on the theology of the Wisdom Literature, see Bruce K. Waltke, *The Book of Proverbs: Chapters 1–15*, New International Commentary on the Old Testament (Grand Rapids: Eerdmans, 2004), 63–133.
13. Martin, *James*, lxxxvii–xc; cf. Dan G. McCartney, "The Wisdom of James the Just," *The Southern Baptist Journal of Theology* 4, no. 3 (Fall 2000): 52–64.

The Teachings of Jesus

James's teachings and thought-world are clearly rooted in the Old Testament. They are also deeply rooted in the teachings of Jesus. Douglas Moo asserts, "No New Testament document is more influenced by the teaching of Jesus than James."[14] The teachings of Jesus are seen in virtually every section and theme of James. Dean Deppe notes 175 different allusions claimed by fifty-three scholars since the beginnings of critical scholarship.[15]

In what way does James reflect the teachings of Jesus?[16] That James heard some of Jesus' teaching and was aware of oral traditions is probable from the frequency of thought parallels.[17] William Baker observes:

> What is so striking to everyone is that James never overtly tags any of his numerous allusions to Jesus' teaching nor even sayings that are very near to quotations, like James 5:12, as being from Jesus. Jesus' teaching appears to have gone long past memorization on the part of the author and likely the readers as well. It has become integrated into the teaching of the author himself. This is no mere rabbinic student reciting verbatim the teaching of his respected mentor. This is a mature teacher himself who is so familiar with Jesus' teaching that it interlaces his speech like the words of torah. More than that, the audience in view is assumed to be mature enough as disciples of Jesus to be so immersed in Jesus' words that they have no need to be coached regarding the allusions either.[18]

14. Douglas J. Moo, *The Letter of James*, Pillar New Testament Commentary (Grand Rapids: Eerdmans, 2000), 27.

15. William R. Baker, "Christology in the Epistle of James," *Evangelical Quarterly* 74, no. 1 (2002): 52n21. Baker cites Dean Deppe, "The Sayings of Jesus in the Epistle of James" (PhD thesis, Free University of Amsterdam, 1996).

16. Concerning the relationship of James to the synoptic problem, Matthew, Luke, Q, Peter, and source theory, see James B. Adamson, *James: The Man and His Message* (Grand Rapids: Eerdmans, 1989), 169–94; Peter H. Davids, "James and Jesus," in *Gospel Perspectives, Volume 5: The Jesus Tradition Outside the Gospels*, ed. David Wenham (Sheffield: JSOT, 1985), 63–84; P. J. Hartin, *James and the Q Sayings of Jesus*, Journal for the Study of the New Testament, Supplement Series 47 (Sheffield: JSOT, 1991).

17. Peter H. Davids, *The Epistle of James*, New International Greek Testament Commentary (Grand Rapids: Eerdmans, 1982), 49. This seems to support an early date.

18. Baker, "Christology in the Epistle of James," 52.

Beyond displaying similarities to the teachings of Jesus in his words, phrases, style, and convictions, James also underlines common themes: wisdom, consistency or hypocrisy, persecution and suffering, rich and poor, faith and works, love and mercy, prayer, and word and law.

More specifically, James's message often comes across as an extension of the teachings of Jesus in the Sermon on the Mount or Sermon on the Plain (Matt. 5–7; Luke 6). Bruce Metzger believes that "Luther was right in applying the criterion 'whatever promotes Christ is apostolic,' but wrong in not recognizing that the epistle of James also 'promotes Christ' by its practical application of the Sermon on the Mount."[19]

In order to communicate the historical order (that James received his material from Jesus) and to show how often James's teaching seems to echo the Sermon on the Mount, I will outline the parallel teaching according to the order of the Sermon on the Mount (Matt. 5–7) and make reference to Matthew first and James second. (I will also reference Luke if his account is closer.)[20]

- The poor as recipients of the kingdom (Matt. 5:3; Luke 6:20; James 2:5)
- A call for mourning (Matt. 5:4; Luke 6:25; James 4:9)
- Praise of meekness (Matt. 5:5; James 3:13–18)
- Mercy given to the merciful (Matt. 5:7; James 2:13)
- Purity of heart (Matt. 5:8; James 4:8)
- Praise of peacemaking (Matt. 5:9; James 3:18)
- Joy in trials and persecution (Matt. 5:10–12; James 1:2)
- Prophets as examples of perseverance through trials (Matt. 5:12; James 5:10–11)
- God as Father (Matt. 5:16, etc.; James 1:17)
- Perfection and unity of the law (Matt. 5:17–19; James 1:25; 2:8–11)

19. Bruce M. Metzger, *The Canon of the New Testament* (Oxford: Clarendon, 1987), 244.

20. Especially helpful in making these lists were Davids, *James*, 47–48; Mahony, "Origin of Jacobean Thought," 233–44.

- The seriousness of a seemingly small infraction of the law (Matt. 5:19; James 2:10)
- The unrighteousness of anger (Matt. 5:22; James 1:20)
- Lust and the course of sin (Matt. 5:27–30; James 1:13–15)
- The prohibition of oaths (Matt. 5:34–37; James 5:12)
- The expectation of nonresistance (Matt. 5:39; James 5:1–6)
- The demand for perfection (Matt. 5:48; James 1:4; 3:2)
- Condemnation of religious hypocrisy (Matt. 6:1–18; James 1:26–27; 2:14–26; a central theme throughout both)
- The decay (by moths and rust or corrosion) of stored-up wealth (Matt. 6:19–20; James 5:2–4)
- The rejection of dual eyes, two masters, and double-mindedness (Matt. 6:22–24; James 1:8; 4:8)
- The transitory nature of life (Matt. 6:34; James 4:13–16)
- The command against judging (Matt. 7:1; James 4:11–12)
- Our judging of others affecting how God judges us (Matt. 7:1–2; James 2:13)
- Asking God in prayer and receiving; overall theology of prayer (Matt. 7:7–8; James 1:5; 4:2–3)
- God as good and the giver of good gifts (Matt. 7:9–11; James 1:17)
- Character depicted as fruit (Matt. 7:16–20; James 3:10–18)
- Fruit (figs and grapes) as consistent with type of tree or root (Matt. 7:16–19; James 3:12)
- Severe future judgment of the wicked (Matt. 7:16–27; James 5:1–6)
- The danger of mere profession (Matt. 7:21–23; James 1:26–27; 2:14–26)
- True followers of Christ hearing and doing (Matt. 7:24–27; James 1:22–25; 2:14–26; a central theme throughout both)
- True followers of Christ persevering through trials (Matt. 7:24–27; James 1:2–8; 5:7–11)

The outline above demonstrates not only that James's teaching is significantly related to Jesus', but also that continuities are found with *every* major section of Jesus' Sermon on the Mount.

But James's teaching reflects more of Jesus' overall teaching than just the Sermon on the Mount. In order to show how frequently James does this, I will outline the similarities according to the order of material in James. This material is not confined to the Sermon on the Mount. Some of what is below are actual parallels, some may be echoes, others mild reflections, others extensions, and still others merely the result of a shared cultural and religious context.[21]

- Joy in trials and persecution (James 1:2; Matt. 5:10–12)
- True followers of Christ persevering through trials (James 1:2–8; Matt. 7:24–27)
- The demand for perfection (James 1:4; Matt. 5:48)
- Asking God and receiving (James 1:5; Matt. 7:7–8)
- Asking in faith without doubting (James 1:6; Matt. 21:21)
- The rejection of dual eyes and double-mindedness (James 1:8; Matt. 6:22–24)
- Blessing of the poor; warning to the rich (James 1:9–10; Luke 6:20–24)
- Blessing upon those who persevere through trials (James 1:12; Matt. 10:22)
- Lust and the course of sin (James 1:13–15; Matt. 5:27–30)
- God as Father (James 1:17; Matt. 5:16, etc.)
- God as good and the giver of good gifts (James 1:17; Matt. 7:9–11)
- Salvation as new birth from God (James 1:18; John 3:1–8)
- The unrighteousness of anger (James 1:20; Matt. 5:22)
- The word implanted as a seed (James 1:21; Matt. 13:1–13, 18–23)
- True followers of Christ hearing and doing (James 1:22–25; Matt. 7:24–27)
- The perfection and unity of the law (James 1:25; Matt. 5:17–19)

---

21. For a careful analysis of the nature of James's dependence on Jesus' teaching, see Richard Bauckham, *James: Wisdom of James, Disciple of Jesus the Sage* (London: Routledge, 1999), 29–111.

- The blessing of the obedient in their doing (James 1:25; John 13:17)
- Condemnation of religious hypocrisy (James 1:26–27; Matt. 6:1–18)
- The danger of mere profession (James 1:26–27; Matt. 7:21–23)
- The poor as recipients of the kingdom (James 2:5; Matt. 5:3; Luke 6:20)
- The rich in faith toward God (James 2:5; Luke 12:21)
- Emphasis on the love command in Leviticus 19:18 (James 2:8; Matt. 22:34–40)
- The perfection and unity of the law (James 2:8–11; Matt. 5:17–19)
- The commandments against murder and adultery stressed in the same order and in a judgment context (James 2:8–11; Matt. 5:21–30)
- The seriousness of a seemingly small infraction of the law (James 2:10; Matt. 5:19)
- Our judging of others affecting how God judges us (James 2:13; Matt. 7:1–2)
- Mercy given to the merciful (James 2:13; Matt. 5:7; 18:21–35)
- Final salvation evidenced in feeding, clothing, etc., fellow believers (James 2:14–17; Matt. 25:34–46)
- Condemnation of religious hypocrisy (James 2:14–26; Matt. 6:1–18)
- The danger of mere profession (James 2:14–26; Matt. 7:21–23)
- True followers of Christ hearing and doing (James 2:14–26; Matt. 7:24–27)
- Judgment according to works (James 2:14–26; Matt. 16:27)
- Character depicted as fruit (James 3:10–18; Matt. 7:16–20)
- Fruit (figs and grapes) as consistent with type of tree or root (James 3:12; Matt. 7:16–19)

- The command to show good works (James 3:13; Matt. 5:16)
- Praise of meekness (James 3:13–18; Matt. 5:5)
- Praise of peacemaking (James 3:18; Matt. 5:9)
- Asking God in prayer and receiving (James 4:2–3; Matt. 7:7–8)
- The "world" as an evil sphere (James 4:4; John 15, etc.)
- The rejection of dual eyes, two masters, and double-mindedness (James 4:4–8; Matt. 6:22–24)
- Purity of heart (James 4:8; Matt. 5:8)
- A call for mourning (James 4:9; Matt. 5:4)
- Warning to those who laugh, and call to "mourn and weep" (James 4:9; Luke 6:25)
- The paradox of humility and exaltation (James 4:10; Matt. 23:12; Luke 14:11)
- The command against judging (James 4:11–12; Matt. 7:1)
- The transitory nature of life (James 4:13–16; Matt. 6:34)
- Judgment coming on the rich (James 5:1–6: Luke 6:24–25)
- Severe future judgment of the wicked (James 5:1–6; Matt. 7:16–27)
- The decay (by moths and rust or corrosion) of stored-up wealth (James 5:2–4; Matt. 6:19–20)
- The expectation of nonresistance (James 5:1–6; Matt. 5:39)
- True followers of Christ persevering through trials (James 5:7–11; Matt. 7:24–27)
- The expectation of the Parousia (the coming of the Lord) (James 5:7–8; Matt. 24:3, 27, 37, 39)
- The coming of the Lord "drawing near" (James 5:8; Luke 21:28)
- The nearness of Jesus' coming as standing at the "door" (James 5:9; Matt. 24:33)
- Prophets as examples of perseverance through trials (James 5:10–11; Matt. 5:12)
- The prohibition of oaths (James 5:12; Matt. 5:34–37)
- Elijah and the drought (James 5:17; Luke 4:25)

The influence of the teachings of Jesus on the epistle of James is astounding! There is not one section of the Sermon on the Mount that James does not reflect, and there is not one section of James that does not reflect the teachings of Jesus. Jesus' teachings are indelibly imprinted on James's themes, God-centered theology, and eschatological orientation. He uses those truths to forge his ethical appeals.

3

James's Pastoral Burden: Wisdom for Consistency in the Community

WHAT IS JAMES'S pastoral burden? What is at the heart of his message to these churches? Scholars have offered various proposals: wholeness, faith, obedience, wisdom, caring for the poor, grace, humility, etc. While agreeing that each of these proposals underlines a significant theme in James, I would suggest that multiple integrating concerns lie at the heart of the epistle. Three of them are wisdom, consistency, and community. That wisdom is significant has been noted by many, including Wall, who states: "In my view, wisdom is the orienting concern of this book by which all else is understood: after all, James refers to wisdom as the divine 'word of truth,' which is graciously provided to a faithful people to make sense of their trials and to guide them through those trials in order to insure their future destiny in the new creation."[1] This wisdom orientation has been highlighted by Richard Bauckham and is evident in the structural analysis of Mark Taylor and George Guthrie.[2]

1. Robert W. Wall, "James, Letter of," in *Dictionary of Later New Testament and Its Developments*, ed. Ralph P. Martin and Peter H. Davids (Downers Grove, IL: InterVarsity Press, 1997), 522.

2. Richard Bauckham, *James: Wisdom of James, Disciple of Jesus the Sage* (London: Routledge, 1999), 93–111; Mark E. Taylor and George H. Guthrie, "The Structure of James," *Catholic Biblical Quarterly* 68 (2006): 681–705.

A second integrating concern of James is consistency. Douglas Moo refers to this as wholeness and shows its centrality to James.[3] David Dockery explains how consistency, or true piety, is interwoven with much of James's message:

> James pictures true piety as the direct application of the implanted word in the life of the believer. The result vertically is the submission to and worship of God. The result horizontally is concern for the poor, widows and orphans in distress. The result relationally is living peaceably with others in the church. The result inwardly is the humility, purity and gentleness of character that comes from heavenly wisdom.[4]

The third integrating concern—community—is one that is often missed. The centrality of this should be clear from James's instruction, reproof, correction, and edification of these Diaspora churches. As we will see, James is not writing primarily to encourage a collection of individuals to be wise or consistent, but to urge these churches to be wise and act consistently.[5] The structural analysis of Taylor and Guthrie also points in this direction.

We should understand these three orienting concerns as together forming James's central pastoral burden. James writes this letter to these churches to offer wisdom for consistency in the community. What do I mean by this?

First, by "*wisdom* for consistency in the community," I mean that the letter of James has roots in the Old Testament wisdom tradition and seeks to dispense wisdom to achieve practical results. As David Hubbard notes, "Wisdom takes insights gleaned from the knowledge of God's ways and applies them in the daily

---

3. Douglas J. Moo, *The Letter of James*, Pillar New Testament Commentary (Grand Rapids: Eerdmans, 2000), 43–46.

4. David S. Dockery, "True Piety in James: Ethical Admonitions and Theological Implications," *Criswell Theological Review* 1, no. 1 (Fall 1986): 69.

5. For more on James as a community document, see Donald J. Verseput, "Genre and Story: The Community Setting of the Epistle of James," *Catholic Biblical Quarterly* 62 (2000): 96–110. Kenneth D. Tollefson sees James as a community document designed to help promote "group faith" and "group maturity." See Tollefson, "The Epistle of James as Dialectical Discourse," *Biblical Theology Bulletin* 27 (1997): 62–69.

walk."[6] This approach to wisdom is at the heart of James. James applies the truths about God and covenant faithfulness to such daily issues as trials, temptations, words, wealth, obedience, planning, and brevity of life. In doing so, James stresses that our response to these daily challenges must be consistent with God's person and ways.

Second, by "wisdom *for consistency* in the community," I mean that James offers wisdom for a purpose: to encourage the covenant faithfulness of the people of God. James's frequent opposition to being double-minded and his regular call for wholeness and integrity apply this wisdom. The goal of wisdom is maturity, completeness (cf. 1:4), and integrity—what we are calling consistency.

Third, "wisdom for consistency *in the community*" means that James is addressing church matters from a pastoral perspective. As a major leader in the Jerusalem church, and therefore of other churches related to that mother church, James was keenly aware of church needs and problems. Indeed, he was deeply involved with them. So he wrote a letter that spoke to the real-life concerns faced by the Diaspora churches. Reading James with pastoral eyes reveals this community emphasis. These Jewish Christians belonged to local congregations (2:2) with teachers (3:1), elders (5:14), and members in need of church leaders' prayers (5:14–16). These believers were experiencing trials (1:2–3) and oppression (2:6; 5:1–11). Some were claiming they had faith, but had little concern for personal holiness (1:22–25; 4:4) and failed to assist the poor (1:26–27; 2:14–17). The congregations also included some who were seeking to gain power as teachers, but were spiritually unqualified for the role (3:1–18). Some, including many desiring to be teachers, were quarrelsome, bringing friction rather than peace (3:13–4:10). James addresses such church problems by offering wisdom for consistency in the community.

Yet the majority of sermons and commentaries on James neglect this community emphasis. I must confess that I made

6. David A. Hubbard, "Wisdom," in *The Illustrated Bible Dictionary*, ed. J. D. Douglas (Downers Grove, IL: InterVarsity Press, 1980), 1650.

this error myself—and did so while serving as a pastor! The first two times I preached through the epistle of James, most of my sermons focused on the individual applications of the exhortations—facing trials at a personal level, dealing with temptation at a personal level, individual obedience with reference to words, etc. While those sermons were not necessarily incorrect, they only shed light on a small portion of James's burden. Regrettably, it was not until the last sermon I preached in my second series on James that I noticed its community-centered perspective. Since that time, however, it has become increasingly clear to me that James is writing pastorally with an emphasis on the covenant community, dealing with church problems, and thinking from the perspective of church leadership.[7]

Interestingly, James's burden resonates with recent proposals in contemporary theology. Evangelicals such as Kevin Vanhoozer suggest that the major aim of theology is wisdom and that the primary context for theology is the covenant community.[8] This reclaiming of theology as offering wisdom for the churches dovetails well with James's pastoral purpose.

"Wisdom for consistency in the community" works well as an integrating center because it makes sense of the obvious emphases of the letter and because it is intimately connected to and shapes other major themes in James: suffering, the poor and the rich, and speech. While saving the details for their respective chapters, we note here how suffering, the poor, and speech are linked to wisdom for consistency in the community. For instance, James instructs exploited church members to choose joy in the midst of their pain because God uses it to bring about their maturity (1:2–11). They should ask God for wisdom, and they must do so in faith. He then clarifies: ask not with an inconsistent, double-minded faith, but with a consistent, single-minded faith. Here we have the theme of suffering driven by the community context,

7. Christopher W. Morgan and B. Dale Ellenburg, *James: Wisdom for the Community* (Fearn, UK: Christian Focus Publications, 2008).
8. Kevin J. Vanhoozer, *The Drama of Doctrine: A Canonical-Linguistic Approach to Christian Theology* (Louisville, KY: Westminster John Knox, 2005), 1–34, 115–50.

linked to the congregational need for wisdom, and coupled with James's call for consistency.

Similarly, the theme of the poor is tied to wisdom and/or consistency in James 1:5–11, 1:22–27, 2:1–13, and 2:14–26. James teaches that wisdom leads to an eschatological perspective in which the righteous poor are vindicated (1:5–11), that consistency is linked to the treatment of the poor (1:22–27), that the poor constitute important members of the community (2:1–13), and that true faith leads to mercy for the poor (2:14–26).

The theme of speech is also shaped by James's pastoral burden to share wisdom for consistency in the community. The congregations have people who presume to be leaders and seek the prominent role of the teacher (3:1). So James reminds them of the extraordinary power of words and the necessity of controlling one's tongue (3:2–12). He points to the inconsistency of blessing God and cursing people, showing that those who assert themselves to be teachers, yet slander the family of God, are inconsistent and hypocritical (3:9–12). James then contrasts wisdom from God with wisdom from below. He shows that God's wisdom is pure, peaceable, humble, and self-giving, whereas worldly wisdom is concerned to promote self and win at all costs (3:13–18). Again and again we find prominent themes shaped by the giving of wisdom and the purpose of leading these congregations to be consistent.

To highlight how central this community concern is in James, let us restate some of the message of James using imperatives (as James loves to do), as if it were given in the form of direct address to the church. In doing so, we better sense the strong community emphasis and James's wisdom for consistency in the community.

- Churches of the Diaspora, when you undergo trials from the rich who are oppressing you, choose joy, have a single-minded faith in God for wisdom, and endure (1:1–12).
- Churches of the Diaspora, repent of your pride and anger. Instead, listen, be patient, and humbly receive the word (1:19–21).

- Churches of the Diaspora, do not merely hear the word or be religious, but obey the word, control your words, take care of the oppressed, and be holy (1:22–27).
- Churches of the Diaspora, do not show favoritism toward the rich who exploit you, but show love and respect to the poor (2:1–13).
- Churches of the Diaspora, do not believe that you are saved by a faith that does not lead you to show love to the hurting. Show your faith by works of love (2:14–26).
- Churches of the Diaspora, do not let people be teachers or leaders who are verbally divisive and destructive (3:1–12).
- Churches of the Diaspora, do not believe those who claim to be wise, but are divisive. Their so-called wisdom is not from God, but from hell (3:13–18).
- Churches of the Diaspora, why are you fighting? Stop trying to get your own way. Stop wanting to be made much of. Stop slandering and judging your fellow brothers and sisters. Instead, repent, be humble, and recognize that there is only one Judge and Lawgiver (4:1–12).
- Churches of the Diaspora, persevere during this period of oppression. God will judge the wicked, rich oppressors with severity. Their time is coming (5:1–12).
- Churches of the Diaspora, stop grumbling against each other. You will be judged, too (5:9).
- Churches of the Diaspora, live in community with one another. Pray for those who are in need. Praise the Lord when others are happy. Pray for healing when someone is sick. Confess your sins to one another. Do all you can to restore those who have wandered away from the truth (5:13–20).

In the Old Testament wisdom tradition, James the sage dispenses wisdom. But even more, James the pastor offers wisdom for consistency in the covenant communities.

With this integrative concern in mind, we will attempt to survey the following major and selected themes in James: wisdom, consistency, suffering, the poor, words, and God's word and law. For the most part, the next several chapters summarize James's teaching on these themes and ground tenets related to them upon specific passages in James. To avoid reading wisdom for consistency in the community into the texts, each theme will be examined separately on its own merits. Yet because some of these themes and tenets are interconnected, and because many passages address multiple themes, some redundancy will be inevitable—and even helpful, making their interrelationships more striking.

4

Wisdom

SINCE JAMES REFLECTS Old Testament wisdom literature and his pastoral burden is to offer wisdom for consistency in the community, the question arises: what does he teach about wisdom? James 1:5–8 and 3:13–18 are particularly rich with his teachings, conveying four principles:

- Living in the Present Age, God's People Need Wisdom (1:5–8).
- God Is the Source of Wisdom (1:5–8).
- Faith Is Necessary to Receive Wisdom (1:5–8).
- Wise Teachers Have Integrity and Promote Consistency in the Church (3:13–18).

Living in the Present Age, God's People Need Wisdom (1:5–8)

The Christians to whom James was writing were experiencing various trials (James 1:2–4). While we do not know exactly what those trials were, the rest of the letter indicates that they likely had to do with poor Christians being persecuted by rich oppressors. In a manner that sounds audacious to us, but stands in continuity with the teachings of Jesus and the other apostles (Matt. 5:10–12; Rom. 5:1–5; 1 Peter 1:6–7), James charges his congregations to count it all joy whenever these trials come. Why? Because God is using the trials to make them steadfast,

47

which in time brings "its full effect, that you may be perfect and complete, lacking in nothing" (1:4). The Revised English Bible translates it well: "Let endurance perfect its work in you that you may become perfected."

James teaches that we experience trials because we still live in the present age. The consummation of the ages has not yet occurred; we still await Jesus' coming, the last judgment, and complete victory. And while we live in this imperfect age, we are being made mature. In this way, we live in both the already and the not yet of our salvation. Just as the kingdom of God has already come and yet has not been fully realized, so our salvation has come and yet we still await its full manifestation. James sees the already and the not yet of our salvation as intertwined because God is using trials to produce perfection and completeness in us. We still need to become perfect, and that can happen only through the historical process that develops our faith, steadfastness, and maturity. In fact, James links "lacking in nothing" in verse 4 with "if any of you lacks wisdom" in verse 5. We need wisdom because we experience trials, and also because we are still lacking. We are not yet "lacking in nothing," so we need wisdom to help us become increasingly mature.

God Is the Source of Wisdom (1:5–8)

James also exhorts: "If any of you lacks wisdom, let him ask God" (1:5). Here James stands in the Old Testament and Jewish traditions. Proverbs 2:6 states this profound truth simply: "For the LORD gives wisdom." Proverbs 1:7 clarifies the Old Testament approach to wisdom: "The fear of the LORD is the beginning of knowledge; fools despise wisdom and instruction." Tremper Longman comments on Proverbs 1:7:

> This statement claims there is no knowledge apart from a proper attitude and relationship to Yahweh. Fear of Yahweh is foundational to knowledge. . . . In this way, the book acknowledges the radically relational and theocentric nature of knowledge/

48

wisdom. . . . It is the first thought that makes all other thoughts fall into place. . . . What the prologue makes clear is that the benefits of wisdom are available only to those who have already made a fundamental religious commitment.[1]

So wisdom at its core is theological. It is rightly understanding our place in the cosmos and relating to God accordingly. He is supreme and we are not. We must fear him and "acknowledge our creaturely dependence upon him."[2] This is basic to James's understanding of wisdom.

James also urges us to ask God for wisdom because of who God is and how he gives. Three truths stand out. First, God gives wisdom *generously* (James 1:5). Because God is single-minded and gives generously, we are to ask with single-mindedness, not with double-mindedness (1:6–8).[3] Here James reflects the teaching of Jesus in Matthew 7:7–11, which stresses that we should ask God because he is generous and enjoys giving good gifts to his children. Derek Tidball comments:

> Gerard Hughes highlighted the way in which God is portrayed as generous in the ministry of Jesus. Hughes pointed to the parables and talked of the "foolish prodigality" of a God who leaves ninety-nine sheep to go in search of one lost one. He wrote of the financial imprudence involved in forgiving a debtor who owed ten thousand talents, and, in paying a full day's pay to those who were last minute workers. The miracles of Jesus demonstrate the same generosity. The 180 gallons of excellent quality wine produced at the wedding in Cana seems "an unnecessarily large quantity," especially at the tail end of the feast. And to feed five thousand and have twelve baskets full of food left over seemed extravagant. "The Father," Hughes concludes, "is presented as a God of

1. Tremper Longman III, *Proverbs*, Baker Commentary on the Old Testament (Grand Rapids: Baker, 2006), 100–104.

2. Daniel J. Estes, *Hear, My Son: Teaching and Learning in Proverbs 1–9*, New Studies in Biblical Theology (Grand Rapids: Eerdmans, 1997), 35–39.

3. Douglas J. Moo, *The Letter of James*, Pillar New Testament Commentary (Grand Rapids: Eerdmans, 2000), 58–59.

overflowing goodness, whose one desire is to share what he has with as many as possible."[4]

Second, God gives wisdom generously "to all" (1:5). He is glad to give wisdom. He does not show favoritism or withhold it from people with genuine faith. He is generous in giving wisdom to all people of faith—no matter our age, gender, ethnicity, or socio-economic level. All who recognize who God is and who they are in relationship to him may receive this blessed gift of wisdom.

Third, God gives wisdom generously to all "without reproach" (1:5). He neither has reservations about giving wisdom, nor will he grumble. Indeed, God is the supreme example of a cheerful and ungrudging giver. God wants the best for people, and he knows that what is best for them is humble submission and dependence upon him.

Faith Is Necessary to Receive Wisdom (1:5–8)

God is the source of wisdom, but he gives it only to those who will use it rightly. James asserts, "But let him ask in faith, with no doubting" (1:6). Verse 5 warmly exhorts readers to seek wisdom from God, but verse 6 adds a stipulation: faith is prerequisite for receiving God's gift of wisdom. Wisdom rightly acknowledges the sovereignty of God and humanity's consequent place in the order of things. Thus, wisdom is inevitably linked to humility and faith.

James explains that to ask in faith is to ask "with no doubting" (1:6). This clarifies the nature and importance of faith. Doubting displays a lack of faith. It is to fail to believe, trust, or rely upon God; it is to be divided and drawn in two directions. Verse 8 describes this condition as being "double-minded." Those who doubt are like "a wave of the sea that is driven and tossed by the

---

4. Derek Tidball, *Wisdom from Heaven: The Message of the Letter of James for Today* (Fearn, UK: Christian Focus Publications, 2003), 41. Tidball references Gerard W. Hughes, *God of Surprises* (London: Darton, Longman and Todd, 1985), 115.

wind," because they drift in accordance with external pressures. James warns such doubters not to think they "will receive anything from the Lord" (1:7). God loves to give wisdom to those who ask, indeed to all who ask, and he loves to give it generously and without any desire to hold back. But he gives wisdom only to those who ask in faith—those who, as the writer of Hebrews states, "believe that he exists and that he rewards those who seek him" (Heb. 11:6). The doubter is "a double-minded man, unstable in all his ways" (James 1:8). "Double-minded" translates *dipsychos*, a term found in the New Testament only here and in 4:8. Its root is "two-souled" or "divided soul." It is to be "two-faced" and indicates covenant unfaithfulness. It is an expression in James that recalls Jesus' teaching on hypocrisy. It is a key term in James and will be discussed in more detail when we look at the theme of consistency.

Since the purpose of wisdom is to enable believers to follow God as a way of life, God grants it only to those who are committed to following him. Why give wisdom to people who will not use it? Those who are interested only in dabbling will be disappointed. Wisdom and faith are intertwined, and both demonstrate covenant faithfulness. Peter Davids puts it frankly: "The man who expects to get something from God despite his lack of commitment is simply deluded."[5] Davids later states:

> The author, then, concludes his description of this doubter with a strong condemnation: his divided mind, when it comes to trusting God, indicates a basic disloyalty toward God. Rather than being a single-minded lover of God, he is one whose character and conduct is unstable, even hypocritical. No wonder he should expect nothing from God! He is not in the posture of a trusting child. For James there is no middle ground between faith and no faith; such a one, he will later argue (4:8), needs to repent.[6]

5. Peter H. Davids, *The Epistle of James*, New International Greek Testament Commentary (Grand Rapids: Eerdmans, 1982), 74.
6. Ibid., 75.

Wise Teachers Have Integrity and Promote Consistency in the Church (3:13-18)

James teaches directly on the subject of wisdom again in 3:13–18. This passage continues the argument in 3:1–12 concerning those seeking to be teachers.[7] These people carry a serious responsibility and need wisdom to know what to say and how to say it. The disaster caused by church leaders using their words unwisely is often enormous, as dreadful as a forest fire or deadly poison. So James helps churches see what good leadership is like by contrasting genuine wisdom with counterfeit wisdom. To show that true wisdom (like true faith) is ethical,[8] James highlights truths about false wisdom and true wisdom, distinguishing them by their characteristics, sources, and results.

James begins the discussion by asking rhetorically, "Who is wise and understanding among you?" (3:13). He then answers his own question: "By his good conduct let him show his works in the meekness of wisdom" (3:13). The point is clear: true, godly wisdom displays itself in consistent Christian behavior, "in the meekness of wisdom."

James then exposes the opposite of true wisdom. Those who long to be viewed as church leaders but exhibit "bitter jealousy and selfish ambition" show that they lack real wisdom. God-given wisdom is meek. It is not linked to envy, rivalry, or self-promotion. It rejects factions, rivalries, or party spirits. People characterized by false wisdom seek to "win" against others, and in so doing they divide churches. If people boast about their wisdom and their power over others, they deny the truth that they supposedly teach, and their so-called wisdom "is not the wisdom that comes down from above, but is earthly, unspiritual, demonic" (3:15). Instead of taking pride in their supposed wisdom, those aspiring to be teachers and leaders should be examining the actual sources of

---

7. See Luke Timothy Johnson, "Reading Wisdom Wisely," *Louvain Studies* 28 (2003): 99–112.

8. See Dan G. McCartney, "The Wisdom of James the Just," *The Southern Baptist Journal of Theology* 4, no. 3 (Fall 2000): 56.

it. Their wisdom is not from above (God), but at best it is earthly and unspiritual, and at worst it is demonic.

James calls the churches' attention to the results of this spurious wisdom: "For where jealousy and selfish ambition exist, there will be disorder and every vile practice" (3:16).

False wisdom is accompanied by damage to churches. When such "jealousy" and "selfish ambition" are present, the outcome includes "disorder and every vile practice" (3:16). James has used the word "disorder" twice already (in 1:8 and 3:8) to describe an unstable man and a restless tongue. Here he points to the restlessness, disorder, and chaos produced by worldly wisdom. If there is chaos in the church, it is likely associated with people promoting themselves for leadership who are not spiritually qualified for it. Such people exhibit false wisdom and the envy, pride, and self-promotion that go with it.[9]

James uses the word "but" to transition to his discussion of the source, characteristics, and results of true wisdom. Unlike the bogus wisdom, true wisdom comes "from above," from God (3:15). Ralph Martin observes, "Strictly speaking James describes what true wisdom results in rather than what it *is*."[10] In a manner that resembles Jesus' beatitudes in the Sermon on the Mount (Matt. 5:3–12) or the apostle Paul's depiction of the fruit of the Spirit (Gal. 5:22–24), James here specifies characteristics of this true wisdom from God that is so vital to the health of these churches: "But the wisdom from above is first pure, then peaceable, gentle, open to reason, full of mercy and good fruits, impartial and sincere" (3:17).

The wisdom that God gives is "first pure," free from the mixed motives that mark the double-minded.[11] True wisdom loves peace and is gentle or noncombative. It is also conciliatory, open to

9. James fostered unity in Acts 15 and 21:18–25. Unity may come from dialogue, but also from rebuking sin. See J. A. Motyer, *The Message of James*, Bible Speaks Today (Downers Grove, IL: InterVarsity Press, 1985), 135.

10. Ralph P. Martin, *James*, Word Biblical Commentary (Waco, TX: Word, 1988), 133.

11. Davids, *James*, 154. He calls these fruits of wisdom "community-preserving virtues" (p. 54).

reason, not self-seeking, and ready to yield to others (cf. Phil. 2:3). Not surprisingly, it is also "full of mercy and good fruits." Being "full of mercy" suggests one who is eager to help and minister to others (cf. 2:12–17). "Good fruits" refers to the good works that a righteous person will exhibit (cf. 2:14–26; Matt. 7:17–20). The fruit discloses the root; the tree will bear fruit in keeping with its nature. The last two descriptions of this wisdom from God are "impartial" and "sincere." "Impartial" occurs only here in the New Testament and refers to one who shows no favoritism, who is consistent in the treatment of people (cf. 2:1–11); people of godly wisdom do not waver in their convictions, depending on the circumstances. To be "sincere," the opposite of hypocritical, is to be undivided, genuine, and integrated.

James concludes this section by pointing to wisdom's results: "And a harvest of righteousness is sown in peace by those who make peace" (3:18). That righteousness is directly related to peace comes as no surprise, as James writes to churches that are marked by pride, slander, and power plays. Those who love peace sow peace, a quality needed in every church.

Teachers reveal by their tongues what kind of wisdom they possess. Not everyone who wants to lead should, because not everyone possesses genuine wisdom. The church should resist those seeking to teach who lack such wisdom. In time, their selfish motives will only cause factions and disorder. They will deem it more important to feel important than to serve the body. Genuine Christian teachers, however, though not perfect (3:2), are deeply concerned about truth and setting a good example (3:13). They humbly plant seeds of truth in peace and produce a harvest of practical righteousness in people's lives. In sum, wise teachers are consistent. They promote consistency in the community, the nature of which we examine next.

5

Consistency

THROUGHOUT HIS LETTER, James offers wisdom so that the churches will be consistent. Calling this "wholeness," Douglas Moo suggests that it is James's primary theme.[1] Notice how pervasive this theme is:

- When you endure trials, choose joy, have faith, and recognize God's work in your maturation (1:2–4).
- When you pray for wisdom, ask in faith; do not waver, be double-minded, or be unstable (1:5–8).
- When you are tempted, do not blame God (he is good), but look at your heart (1:13–18).
- Do not only listen to the word, but also obey it (1:22–25).
- If you are genuine in religion, you will control your tongue, take care of the oppressed, and be holy (1:26–27).
- If you claim to keep the royal law of love, then treat the poor with respect and mercy (2:1–13).
- Do not only claim to have faith, but also demonstrate your faith by good works and love for others (2:14–26).
- Do not claim to praise God with the very tongue with which you curse people, but control your words and use them to edify and not destroy (3:1–12).

---

1. Douglas J. Moo, *The Letter of James*, Pillar New Testament Commentary (Grand Rapids: Eerdmans, 2000), 46; cf. Craig L. Blomberg and Mariam J. Kamell, *James*, Zondervan Exegetical Commentary on the New Testament (Grand Rapids: Zondervan, 2008), 261–62; T. B. Cargal, *Restoring the Diaspora: Discursive Structure and Purpose in the Epistle of James* (Atlanta: Scholars Press, 1993), 98–118.

- If you claim to be wise, then show it by a good life, filled with humility, consideration of others, and love for peace (3:13–18).
- If you want to be exalted, do not exalt yourselves, but submit yourselves humbly to God, repent of your sin, and live right (4:1–10).
- If you claim to care about the law, then do not slander and judge others; by doing such things, you break the law (4:11–12).
- If you know to do what is good, then do it; otherwise, it is sin (4:13–17).
- Do not grumble or swear, for you too will be judged (5:1–12).

Time after time, James calls for such integrity and essentially asserts: "Stop saying one thing and doing something else. Stop claiming to have faith and yet not be trusting God in your trials. Listen to the word *and* obey it. Do not presume you are religious if you do not take care of the oppressed. Do not claim to keep the law of love while the whole time you treat the poor with disrespect. Do not claim to praise God with the very tongue with which you curse people made in his image. Do not claim to revere the law while you slander others. Do not merely claim to have faith; demonstrate it!" Throughout his epistle, James opposes duplicity and double-mindedness and calls for holistic Christianity—churches actually living out the gospel, not just claiming to embrace it.

While James's emphasis on consistency in the church and the Christian life is integrated throughout the entire letter, certain texts highlight his related teachings (1:5–8; 1:22–27; 2:14–26; 3:9–12; 4:7–10) and reveal important principles about consistency:

- Consistency Is Linked to Wisdom and Faith (1:5–8).
- Consistency Is Contrasted with Double-mindedness (1:5–8).
- Consistency Is a Way of Life, Not Merely Religious Activity (1:22–27).
- Consistency Will Be Blessed by the Lord (1:22–27).

- Consistency Is a Fruit of True Faith (2:14–26).
- Consistency and Inconsistency Are Revealed in Words (3:9–12).
- Consistency Is Demanded by God (4:7–10).

Consistency Is Linked to Wisdom and Faith (1:5–8)

We examined James 1:5–8 with a focus on wisdom, but it also reveals much about James's teaching on consistency. James contrasts faith with doubting, which he pictures as tossing about like a wave in the sea. To ask God for wisdom without faith is inconsistent. Wisdom is given for the purpose of helping us be faithful to God and his covenant, so if we are unfaithful or indifferent to being faithful, we contradict ourselves in asking for wisdom. Consistency is necessary for the reception of wisdom and for answered prayer (4:1–4).

Consistency Is Contrasted with Double-mindedness (1:5–8)

As mentioned earlier, "double-minded" translates *dipsychos*, a term found in the New Testament only in James 1:8 and 4:8. Moo wonders if James "coined the term to accentuate his concern that believers display a wholehearted, consistent, and integral faith commitment to God."[2] To be double-minded is to have divided loyalties and indicates covenant unfaithfulness.[3] Luke Johnson explains: "What makes someone double-minded is precisely the desire to live by both measures at once, to be friends with everyone [the world and God]."[4]

---

2. Moo, *James*, PNTC, 62.

3. David DeGraaf suggests that "with no doubt" is an inadequate translation and prefers, "without divided loyalties and divisive attitudes." His contention about divided loyalties fits James, but the point about divisive attitudes seems a stretch. See DeGraaf, "Some Doubts about Doubt: The New Testament Use of *Diakrino*," *Journal of the Evangelical Theological Society* 48, no. 4 (December 2005): 733–55, especially 741–42.

4. Luke Timothy Johnson, "Friendship with the World/Friendship with God: A Study of Discipleship in James," in *Discipleship in the New Testament*, ed. Fernando F. Segovia (Philadelphia: Fortress, 1985), 182–83.

Although the term "double-minded" is unusual, the concept is not, as Moo points out. The Psalms, for example, bless those who follow God with "their whole heart" (Ps. 119:2) and condemn those who speak with "a double heart" (Ps. 12:2; cf. Hos. 10:2). Jesus himself appeals to Deuteronomy 6:5 and its call to love God holistically: "You shall love the Lord your God with all your heart and with all your soul and with all your mind" (Matt. 22:37). He also discusses seeking first the kingdom, serving only one master, having a single eye, and the sin of hypocrisy (Matt. 6:19–34).

Moo also notes that multiple Old Testament and Jewish texts stress the "two ways" tradition, which forces a choice between two options, shaping one's eternal destiny. For example, one Jewish text states, "Woe to timid hearts and slack hands, to the sinner who walks along two ways!" (Sirach 2:12).[5] The book of Proverbs instructs the young, morally unformed man to follow the way of Yahweh, often presented as the "woman" wisdom, and to avoid the path of the "woman" folly (idolatry, empty gods, and all competing voices). Jesus often gives similar counsel: we must choose his way, the way of the kingdom. We cannot have two masters, take two roads, bear two fruits, or lay two foundations (Matt. 7:13–27).

Double-minded living is spiritual wavering, trying to live a double life, seeking to follow a double standard, wanting to please two masters, seeking to walk along two paths, or claiming to be religious without covenant faithfulness. In contrast, consistency for James embraces purity, single-minded devotion, integrity, sincerity, and wholeness—covenant faithfulness.

Consistency Is a Way of Life, Not Merely Religious Activity (1:22–27)

James 1:18–21 speaks of the word of God bringing forth a new creation and urges people to receive the word with meekness. James 1:22–27 spells out what it means to hear and accept

---

5. Quoted by Moo, *James*, PNTC, 62–63.

the word: to practice it as a way of life. We should not minimize how important it is to hear the word; James himself bases many of his commands on it. But James knew that those to whom he was writing neither rejected the word in principle nor neglected to hear it. No, their problem, like that of so many, was that they loved religious activities, but failed to live out the reality behind those activities.

Jesus speaks against the same tendency. In his conclusion to the Sermon on the Mount, he demands the producing of good fruit (Matt. 7:15–20). Obedience to his commands is necessary for entrance into his kingdom (7:21–23). The hearing and doing of his words is the essence of building on the right foundation (7:24–27). Likewise, in Luke 11:28, Jesus asserts, "Blessed rather are those who hear the word of God and keep it!"

Several years ago, Chuck Swindoll illustrated this recurring religious tendency to hear the word without doing it. Here is a summary of his story, which captures this tendency and its fundamental absurdity:

> Let's pretend that . . . you are my executive assistant in a company that is growing rapidly. I'm the owner and I'm interested in expanding overseas. To pull this off, I make plans to travel abroad and stay there until the new branch office gets established. . . . I leave you in charge of the busy stateside organization. I tell you that I will write you regularly and give you direction and instructions. . . .
>
> Months pass. A flow of letters are mailed . . . [in which] I spell out all my expectations. Finally, I return. . . . I am stunned!

Swindoll vividly portrays the owner's surprise at the state of the business: grass is uncut, weeds are everywhere, receptionists are doing their nails, trash cans are overflowing, floors are dirty, and well-paid workers are playing games. Irritated, the owner finds the executive assistant and asks,

> "What in the world is going on, man?"
> "What do ya' mean, Chuck?"

"Well, look at this place! Didn't you get any of my letters?"

"Letters? Oh, yeah—sure, got every one of them. As a matter of fact, Chuck, we have had *letter study* every Friday night since you left. We have even divided all the personnel into small groups and discussed many of the things you wrote. Some of those things really were interesting. You'll be pleased to know that a few of us have actually committed to memory some of your sentences and paragraphs. One or two memorized an entire letter or two! Great stuff in those letters!"

"Okay, okay—you got my letters, you studied them and meditated on them, discussed and even memorized them. *BUT WHAT DID YOU DO ABOUT THEM?*"

"Do? Uh—we didn't *do* anything about them."[6]

Hearing God's word without doing it is even more intolerable than such behavior, so James warns against such foolishness and then applies the command to "do the word" to three specific concerns. Genuine Christianity leads to controlling the tongue, showing compassion to those in need, and manifesting moral purity and integrity (1:26–27).

In sum, James begins and ends this section with the assertion that those who are religious but do not practice the word only deceive themselves with a worthless religion (1:22, 26–27). As God is holy, his covenant people should be holy (cf. Lev. 19:2). True religion, one that God accepts as genuine, manifests itself in a life of covenant faithfulness.

Consistency Will Be Blessed by the Lord (1:22–27)

In this sobering passage, James finds a way to encourage the faithful, emphasizing that consistency will be blessed by the Lord. The one who actually does the word—which James calls a mirror that shows what we truly are (1:23), and the perfect law of liberty (1:25)—"will be blessed in his doing"

6. Charles R. Swindoll, *Improving Your Serve: The Art of Unselfish Living* (Waco, TX: Word, 1981), 170–71 (emphasis in original).

(1:25). Here we hear James echoing the words of Jesus again, for "blessed" is the terminology of the Beatitudes. Jesus did not bestow blessedness on the merely religious, but on the poor in spirit, those who mourn, the meek, those who hunger and thirst after righteousness, the merciful, those who are pure in heart, the peacemakers, and those who are persecuted for his sake (Matt. 5:3–12).

James 1:25 likewise promises blessedness to those who are active doers of the word. This recalls James 1:12 and its emphasis on the blessedness of those who persevere. God will bless those who truly follow him. And what a blessing it is that God promises to accept the religion of the consistent, the ones who have genuine faith in Christ!

Consistency Is a Fruit of True Faith (2:14–26)

Consistency, we have seen, is a way of life and more than being religious, but now we raise the stakes: it is also a necessary consequence of true faith. God will not justify those whose faith is in name only and devoid of works. James 2:14–26, which we will address in more detail in the chapter entitled "James and Paul," condemns those whose faith fails to display itself in actions.

James speaks of perfection or maturity as a goal for believers and calls them to good works, but this lifestyle of following God is not optional; it necessarily characterizes all genuine Christians. In other words, good works are not nice additions to our faith, but are necessary corollaries to it. Faith cannot be "by itself," without works accompanying it (2:17) or "apart from works" (2:20, 26), but is active along with works, is completed by works, and displays its reality through works (2:18, 22). For James, grace is prior to faith (1:18; 2:5), and faith is prior to works (2:14–26). But this does not mean that works are optional. Not at all. Genuine faith is expressed through consistency in life and deeds.

Consistency and Inconsistency Are Revealed in Words (3:9–12)

Inconsistent words display an inconsistent heart. Just as James 2:14–26 shows that genuine faith expresses itself in good *works*, James 3:9–12 reveals that genuine faith expresses itself in good *words*. As James 2:14–26 stresses the incongruity of words without action, James 3:9–12 displays the inconsistency of blessing God while simultaneously cursing people. And whereas James 2:14–26 portrays people who express kind words to the hurting, but fail to back them up with works of mercy, so James 3:9–12 depicts people who express kind words to God, but hurtful words to those created in his image.

Writing primarily to the community of faith, James states that the tongue can stain individuals and churches (cf. 3:2, 4). Ralph Martin is helpful here: "The implication is that by irresponsible speech the whole body of Christ is stained."[7] All pastors and church leaders can attest to James's burden. Churches are seriously hurt by careless tongues wielded by inconsistent and double-minded people. The oddity is that the most vicious speech frequently comes from the mouths of people who claim to love God. James 3:9–12 points out this absurd inconsistency: the same tongue is used to praise God and slander people who are created in his image.

Again James reflects the teachings of the Old Testament and of Jesus. Jesus applies Isaiah 29:13 to the scribes and Pharisees, who were famous for their meticulous religious observance: "This people honors me with their lips, but their heart is far from me; in vain do they worship me" (Matt. 15:8). Jesus then asserts that it is not what enters the mouth that makes someone unclean, but what comes out of it; and what comes out reveals the unclean heart that produces it (15:10–20).

James points out this inconsistency with rhetorical questions and three examples: a fountain that produces both fresh and bitter water, a fig tree yielding olives, and a vine with figs (3:11–12). The idea is that root determines fruit; the produce reveals the nature

---

7. Ralph P. Martin, *James*, Word Biblical Commentary (Waco, TX: Word, 1988), 115.

of its source (cf. Jesus' teaching in Matt. 7:16–20; 12:33–35; Luke 6:43–45). In this way, James drives home his point: sinful words come from sinful hearts, and people who genuinely love God display their basic consistency in following God, even in the difficult arena of speech (cf. 3:2).

Consistency Is Demanded by God (4:1–10)

James 4:1–10 is a sobering call for repentance, rebuking some in the churches for their pride, quarrelling, and selfish praying. James then calls them spiritual adulterers, friends with the world, enemies of God, proud, unclean, sinners, and double-minded. Such hypocrisy damages the church and undercuts its ability to shine as light in the world.

James does not give up on such people, but urges them to repent. Authentic repentance is displayed through acknowledging our creaturely dependence on God and his will. It manifests itself in resisting the ways of the devil—pride, slander, and self-promotion—and in approaching God with a humble, broken spirit. Amazingly, God receives and exalts us when we genuinely repent. He also uses us to foster wholeness in the church.

Suffering

A THIRD MAJOR THEME in James is suffering. In a pastoral manner, James wrote to churches that had experienced much suffering and testing. What types of suffering did they face? James began his letter by noting their "various" trials—all types of unexpected tests (1:2). Some were "suffering" (5:13). There was also widespread poverty, some of which was severe, illustrated by the need of food and clothing (2:16). Many were persecuted, prosecuted (2:5–6), oppressed, and exploited by the wealthy (5:1–11). They had little political, social, or economic clout to address these concerns. In addition, some were seriously ill (5:14–16). James recognized their difficulties and addressed their situation in several passages: 1:2–12; 1:27; 2:6–7; 2:14–16; 5:1–11; 5:13–16.

While we will look at the particulars of these passages shortly, it is helpful first to get a panoramic view of James's response to suffering. He basically responds in two ways. First, he encourages those who are suffering. Second, he exhorts the church to respond properly to people who are suffering.

In his encouragement of believers who are suffering, James urges them to respond with joy, with the realization that God is producing perseverance in them, and with prayer to God for wisdom. They also should recognize that the wicked rich will be humiliated and the righteous will be exalted, and that God will bless those who endure trials with faith and patience (1:2–12). They should not demean themselves by showing partiality to the oppressors (2:5–7). They should be patient in the midst of suffering, because the Lord knows of it, has not forgotten them, will return to judge, and will ultimately vindicate the righteous and punish the wicked (5:1–11). James later urges those who are suffering to pray (5:13) and those who are sick to call for the elders of the church to pray over them and to confess their sins to each other (5:14–16).

James also advises the church to respond appropriately to the suffering of others. The church is not to show favoritism to the rich, but rather should stand with the poor (2:5–7). The church must not accept mere platitudes as a substitute for the important work of showing love to the hurting, feeding the hungry, and clothing the poor (2:15). The church is to be patient in the midst of suffering because the Lord sees the suffering, the church lives in the already and the not yet, and the Judge will finally set the record straight. In the meantime, Christians must persevere and not grumble at one another (5:1–11). Further, the church leaders should pray for the sick and suffering (5:13–16).

In his encouragement of those who are suffering and in his appeals to the church to help those who are suffering, James offers many insights:

- Suffering Does Come and in Various Forms (1:2–12).
- Suffering Is Not Good, but Is Used by God for Our Good (1:2–12).
- Suffering Is Linked to the Present Age (1:9–12).
- God Will Bless Those Who Persevere through Suffering (1:9–12).
- Churches Must Minister to the Suffering (1:27; 2:6–7; 2:14–26; 5:13–16).
- God Judges All Who Oppress His People (5:1–6).
- Sufferers Must Be Patient (5:7–11).

Suffering Does Come and in Various Forms (1:2-12)

Although too much could be made of it, notice that James does not say "if" you encounter trials, but "when" you do (1:2).

Trials do come to faithful Christians and healthy churches. The proponents of the health and wealth theology need to read afresh passages such as James 1:2–12 and 5:1–8, as well as Romans 5:1–5, 2 Corinthians 1:3–7, 1 Peter 1:5–8, and 2 Timothy 3:12. Christians should not be surprised when they face trials or encounter suffering. The churches receiving James's epistle had been suffering and would continue to suffer.

Sometimes the particular forms of their suffering are not spelled out. For example, James informs us that these believers were experiencing "various" trials—all types of unexpected tests (1:2). By referring to "trials of various kinds," James may be writing vaguely enough to insure that his words apply to those experiencing trials in many forms—physical pain, sickness, death of loved ones, etc.[1] Such general or health-related suffering seems to be his focus in 5:13–16, where he uses the general expression "suffering" (5:13) and speaks of ministering to believers who are seriously ill (5:14–16). "Trials of various kinds" could also refer to the community sufferings he will later mention, including widespread poverty (2:16), persecution (2:5–6), and exploitation (5:1–11).

Suffering Is Not Good, but Is Used by God for Our Good (1:2–12)

While James teaches much about suffering, his intention is pastoral, so he gives most of his attention to helping suffering believers respond appropriately to it. It is important to notice, however, that his pastoral advice is intertwined with his theological perspective. Indeed, according to James, to respond to suffering properly, Christians must know and believe some things about God, suffering, and God's eschatological purposes. To this James devotes much attention.

So what pastoral encouragement does James offer these suffering communities? At first glance, James's "encouragement"

1. Douglas J. Moo, *The Letter of James*, Pillar New Testament Commentary (Grand Rapids: Eerdmans, 2000), 54.

appears shocking, if not downright offensive! He instructs these troubled believers to consider it "all joy" when trials come (1:2–3), to let perseverance work in them (1:4), to ask God for wisdom (1:5–8), to remember to view the rich and the poor from an eternal perspective (1:9–11), and to keep in mind the blessedness that comes from enduring life's trials (1:12).

James first urges his readers who face such circumstances to "count it all joy" (1:2). This is the heart of James's exhortation in 1:2–11. In the Greek text, "joy," the object of the verb, is placed first for emphasis. Believers experiencing such trials are not told simply to "hang in there" or even to be more detached, as a Stoic philosopher would say, but to consider it joy.[2] To those familiar with the New Testament, this is no surprise. Paul's teaching on the matter in Romans 5:1–5 is similar:

> Therefore, since we have been justified by faith, we have peace with God through our Lord Jesus Christ. Through him we have also obtained access by faith into this grace in which we stand, and we rejoice in hope of the glory of God. More than that, we rejoice in our sufferings, knowing that suffering produces endurance, and endurance produces character, and character produces hope, and hope does not put us to shame, because God's love has been poured into our hearts through the Holy Spirit who has been given to us.

Peter likewise stresses joy as the suitable response to trials:

> In this you rejoice, though now for a little while, as was necessary, you have been grieved by various trials, so that the tested genuineness of your faith—more precious than gold that perishes though it is tested by fire—may be found to result in praise and glory and honor at the revelation of Jesus Christ. (1 Peter 1:6–7)

Yet sometimes we are so familiar with the biblical teaching related to suffering that we forget to be surprised by it: count it all

---

2. Peter H. Davids, *The Epistle of James*, New International Greek Testament Commentary (Grand Rapids: Eerdmans, 1982), 67.

joy when you face various trials. Joy? When suffering comes our way, we tend to respond with frustration, or a sense of helplessness, or even fear—but joy? In such times, how is joy a possible response?

It is important to understand what is and what is not intended by James's command here. He is not recommending positive thinking. He is not saying, "I know you are hurting, but be positive. Smile. Don't worry; be happy." James is not offering the glib advice that all too often comes from well-intentioned but unwise people at times such as funerals. Nor is James saying that suffering is good. The community suffering in view in James 1:2–4 seems to be persecution and exploitation by wealthy landowners. If that is the case, then the suffering is a result of the sin of the landowners. Such behavior is castigated later in James 5:1–6. So suffering is not considered good here. In Romans 8:28, the apostle Paul corroborates this. It is not that all things that happen in life are good, but that God works all things together for good to those who love God and are called according to his purpose.

So then, what does James intend? Here, as so often in this epistle, he echoes the teachings of Jesus. In the Sermon on the Mount, Jesus teaches:

> Blessed are those who are persecuted for righteousness' sake, for theirs is the kingdom of heaven. Blessed are you when others revile you and persecute you and utter all kinds of evil against you falsely on my account. Rejoice and be glad, for your reward is great in heaven, for so they persecuted the prophets who were before you. (Matt. 5:10–12; cf. Luke 6:22–23)

When you are persecuted on my behalf, Jesus says, rejoice, for you are blessed (cf. 1 Peter 2:19–23). James's exhortation in 1:2 to consider it all joy, as well as his emphasis in 1:12 on the blessedness of those who persevere through the tests, reiterate Jesus' encouragement to believers.

Not only does James stress the proper response of joy because of the future blessing for those who endure, but he also points to the good by-products of trials. Perseverance, completeness, and blamelessness are produced when people have faith in the midst of suffering (1:3–4; cf. Rom. 5:1–5; 2 Cor. 1:3–7; 1 Peter 1:5–8). James urges rejoicing, "for you know that the testing of your faith produces steadfastness" (1:3). James here associates trials with the testing of faith, which is interesting in light of the context. The trials in view were likely brought on by evil, rich landowners. Yet while these oppressors' sins caused the believers' suffering, James asserts that God is at work, using the suffering as a testing of the faith of his people. Such is the nature of the present age.

What precisely does James mean by "the testing of your faith" (1:3)? He uses a different word here than the one translated "trials" in verse 2. Douglas Moo comments:

> "Testing" translates a rare Greek word (*dokimion*), which is found elsewhere in the New Testament only in 1 Pet. 1:7 and in the Septuagint only in Ps. 11:7 and Prov. 27:21. Peter apparently uses the word to denote the result of testing; the NIV translates "genuine." But the two Old Testament occurrences both denote the process of refining silver or gold, and this is the way James uses the word. The difficulties of life are intended by God to refine our faith: heating it in the crucible of suffering so that impurities might be refined away and so that it might become pure and valuable before the Lord. The "testing of faith" here, then, is not intended to determine whether a person has faith or not; it is intended to purify faith that already exists.[3]

What does this testing do? It develops perseverance (*hypomonē*). This has been translated "perseverance," "endurance," "steadfastness," "fortitude," and "patience." Like a muscle that becomes strong when it faces resistance from a weight, Christians develop spiritual strength and stamina by facing trials. It is hard to imagine how perseverance could be developed in any way other than by such resistance, since perseverance presupposes a pressure to endure. So when trials come, James says, joyfully recognize that God is developing perseverance and other good

3. Moo, *James*, PNTC, 54–55.

traits in you. The development of this perseverance is a process. One event does not bring forth enduring character. It is the real-life process of encountering trials and responding to them in faith that produces perseverance.[4] But perseverance is not only an end; it is also a means to further ends: "And let steadfastness have its full effect, that you may be perfect and complete, lacking in nothing" (1:4). As we view suffering with wisdom and from an eschatological perspective, we discover that it in itself is not the end that God has in mind; our maturity is.

Suffering Is Linked to the Present Age (1:9–12)

James 1:9–11 addresses the destinies of the rich and the poor. The section explains that although the rich oppressors appear to be winning now, in the end they will lose; and although the poor and oppressed seem to be losing now, in the end they will win. As Jesus so often does (e.g., in Luke 16:19–31), James points to a future reversal: the rich exploiters will be brought down and destroyed, but the humble believers will be exalted and blessed (1:9–11; cf. 5:1–8).[5] Despite the fact that the suffering addressed in James 1:2–12 is the result of human evil, believers can rest assured that God providentially guides all history and that they will be faced with no circumstance that he ultimately will not use for their good and his glory (cf. 2 Cor. 4:1–18).

God Will Bless Those Who Persevere through Suffering (1:9–12)

James 1:12 is transitional: "Blessed is the man who remains steadfast under trial, for when he has stood the test he will receive

4. Davids, *James*, 69.

5. This is what I call "the comfort of hell." Biblical writers often point to hell as an encouragement to, and comfort for, persecuted believers. Hell demonstrates that justice will prevail and reminds persecuted believers that they will ultimately be vindicated (cf. 2 Thess. 1:5–11; Rev. 14:9–11; 20:11–15; 21:8).

the crown of life, which God has promised to those who love him." The persevering ones in 1:12 are probably the same people who are characterized as the poor in 1:9–11. As the poor will receive exaltation, the persevering will receive divine approval, even the promised crown of life. The crown spoken of here is compared with a head wreath or garland that was given as a victor's prize in the Greek Olympic games. At times it was given to men whom the community wanted to honor, and it was worn in religious and secular feasts. The persevering ones receive a crown that consists of eternal life, which far surpasses the fading crown of earthly prosperity and fame (cf. Rev. 2:10).

The importance of persevering through trials is striking. James does not say that suffering is good or that trials always produce good results, but, as Dan McCartney observes: "This chain of life in James 1:12 stands in opposition to a chain of death in 1:13–15, where trials lead to desires which give birth to sin, which brings forth death. Again, this shows that it is not the trial itself that produces maturity and life, for a trial could result in non-endurance, in the giving in to desire, and in the birthing of sin and death."[6]

James 1:12 offers hope to the believer because of the covenant promise of true joy and life, and it also warns those undergoing trials to choose the correct path: covenant faithfulness. In so doing, James caps off the other exhortations in 1:2–11 by reminding his readers to rejoice, to let steadfastness have its full effect, to ask God for wisdom, and to view suffering through an eschatological lens.

Churches Must Minister to the Suffering (1:27; 2:6–7; 2:14–26; 5:13–16)

James consistently urges the churches to minister to the suffering. He encourages believers who encounter painful trials,

---

6. Dan G. McCartney, "Suffering and the Apostles," in *Suffering and the Goodness of God*, ed. Christopher W. Morgan and Robert A. Peterson, Theology in Community (Wheaton, IL: Crossway, 2008), 106; cf. Tracy L. Howard, "Suffering in James 1:2–12," *Criswell Theological Review* 1, no. 1 (Fall 1986): 71–84.

but he also wants the people of God to respond to the needs of those who are suffering. McCartney observes:

> Just as genuine faith endures trials, so a Christian must respond to the suffering of others as a fellow sufferer. Hence he says true religion[7] is to care for sufferers (James 1:27). Because real faith (2:14–17) is faith that God will exalt the humble (1:9), the works that proceed from true faith will involve showing mercy to those who suffer. Of particular concern to James are the truly destitute, such as "orphans and widows" (1:27), or the man in filthy garments (2:2), who in that social environment were often the most marginalized and powerless people. The church is the community that anticipates the eschatological reversal by caring for and respecting the poor.

Therefore James has little tolerance for those who show favoritism to the rich. This kind of favoritism is offensive first because it violates the law of love and misrepresents the character of God, who cares about the poor. Note that the context of the law of love in Leviticus 19 specifically condemns partiality (Lev. 19:15).[8] Second, partiality belies the eschatological nature of the community, which ought to display in advance God's exaltation of the poor. James 2:1–17 thus teaches us that faithful living does not just pity the poor, it *respects* the poor. This is a difficult concept for most of us who are not poor, especially because suffering, poverty and destitution can make a person appear repulsive, which in turn has the effect of increasing that person's suffering.[9]

7. McCartney, "Suffering and the Apostles," 107n15 reads: "The term used here for 'religion' (*threskeia*) means not one's overall faith commitments, but religious practice, acts of piety, or cultic activity. By 'true religion,' therefore, James does not mean 'the essence of true Christian faith' but 'the essence of true Christian religious activity.'"

8. Ibid., 107n16 reads: "The love command of Lev. 19:18 is shared throughout the New Testament as definitive for Christian life. Its widespread use as the basis of ethics is probably due to the fact that it was promulgated by Jesus himself (Mark 12:29–31 and parallels). James's point is that showing favoritism violates the most basic ethic of God and, hence, violates the whole law."

9. Ibid., 107 (emphasis in original).

McCartney is right. James demands that the people of God minister to the needs of those suffering, and that they do so in ways that provide the relief needed. The church must protect widows and orphans, respect the poor, and assist the needy. The church and its leaders must pray for the sick, and at times pray over the person who needs to be healed.

The real people of God do more than hear the word, attend services, and know correct doctrine. They display their faith and love for Christ by loving others. James again sounds the note of Jesus in Matthew 25:31–46: those who display their love for Jesus by meeting the needs of his suffering people inherit eternal life, and those who fail to do so receive eternal punishment (cf. Luke 4:18–20; 6:20–26; 16:19–31; 18:18–34).

God Judges All Who Oppress His People (5:1–6)

James the prophet brings the charges, the evidence, and the verdict of God's judgment against the rich oppressors (cf. 1:9–11). Their future is depicted as misery, fire, and a day of slaughter (5:1–6). By speaking of the future judgment awaiting the rich exploiters, James encourages the believing community. And as we will see in the next chapter, oppressed believers can rest assured that God will ultimately vindicate them.

Those Suffering Must Be Patient and Not Grumble against One Another (5:7–11)

In James 5:1–6, James writes as a prophet, denouncing oppression; in 5:7–11, he speaks with the voice of a pastor, heartening and warning the oppressed people of God. Since the judgment of the wicked remains in the future, those who are suffering need instruction on how to live in the meantime. As followers of Christ, they are to be marked by joy, faith, hope, and patience in suffering, not by grumbling against one another.

Their patience is rooted in many things, primarily the coming of the Lord, to which James refers three times in this section (5:7, 8, 9). James also gives three concrete examples to inspire patience: the farmer (5:7), the prophets (5:10), and Job (5:11). Adamson states: "The farmer awaiting the harvest is a familiar Jewish picture of salvation and the last judgment. Like the farmer the Christian must be patient and depend on God to consummate his purpose."[10] James reiterates the command at the beginning of 5:7 to "be patient": just like the farmer, "you also be patient" (5:8). He then adds, "Establish your hearts" (5:8), which is followed by an explanation: be stable in your faith because of the blessed hope of the Lord's coming.

Recalling the Israelites in the wilderness, James insists, "Do not grumble against one another, brothers, so that you may not be judged; behold, the Judge is standing at the door" (5:9). While grumbling may be occasioned by difficult circumstances, it is rooted in pride and ingratitude. Grumbling declares that someone has either not done something that he ought to have done, or that he has done something wrong. When we grumble, therefore, we judge. If, however, we exercise patience and develop Christian stability—with our eyes on the Lord's return—we appreciate that his return will herald the final judgment. In the meantime, we must leave all judgment to the Judge. Few take grumbling seriously. But God does, and so should every Christian who focuses on the Lord's coming. Indeed, the manner in which we judge others in our grumbling against them is the way we shall find ourselves judged (Matt. 7:1–2).

James then points to the prophets who exhibited patience and faithfulness, despite the suffering they endured (5:10; cf. Heb. 11). Elijah was hounded and hated (1 Kings 18:10, 17). Jeremiah was thrown into a cistern and threatened with death by starvation (Jer. 38:1–13). Amos was falsely accused of organizing a conspiracy and was told to go back to where he had come from (Amos 7:10–13). Once more James reflects Jesus'

10. James B. Adamson, *The Epistle of James*, New International Commentary on the New Testament (Grand Rapids: Eerdmans, 1976), 191.

Sermon on the Mount: "Blessed are you when others revile you and persecute you and utter all kinds of evil against you falsely on my account. Rejoice and be glad, for your reward is great in heaven, for so they persecuted the prophets who were before you" (Matt. 5:11–12).

Finally, James presents Job as a specific example of this steadfast endurance in the face of affliction. But the term James uses here is not "patience," as in 5:10, but "steadfastness" (5:11; cf. 1:3–4). Through all his unexplained sufferings, Job was a stellar model of endurance, and despite everything he remained devoted to the Lord (Job 1:21; 2:10; 16:9–21; 19:25–27). A final element of encouragement is offered by "the purpose of the Lord," who remains "compassionate and merciful," faithful to his covenant people.

In sum, James contributes much to our understanding of suffering.[11] He gives us a theological perspective, and he challenges us to action. We should respond to our suffering with joy, faith, perseverance, hope, and caution. And we should respond to the suffering of others with ministry, encouragement, love, and prayer.

---

11. For an examination of suffering from contemporary, biblical, theological, philosophical, and pastoral perspectives, see Christopher W. Morgan and Robert A. Peterson, eds., *Suffering and the Goodness of God* (Wheaton, IL: Crossway, 2008).

7

The Poor

JAMES HAS MUCH to contribute toward our view of wealth and poverty. He stands in the Old Testament tradition of using the term "poor" to refer to the oppressed and often to the righteous. It is not hard to see how this originally financial term came to be applied to those who are powerless or marginalized, and then to those who are oppressed, for the poor are often powerless, and the powerless are often oppressed. Furthermore, the powerless and the oppressed are more likely to recognize their needs and to depend upon God to meet them, and so the term "poor" was further extended to express humility and righteousness. The poor are also identified with the exiled people of God (Isa. 26:6; 49:13; 51:21), who look to him for their ultimate vindication (Isa. 49; 51: 54; 61).[1] This was true for Israel, the Qumran community, and probably James's recipients, the Christian covenant communities of the Dispersion. Thus, the identity of the "poor" in James is hard to pinpoint precisely, but the term seems to combine these connotations:

- financially poor
- marginalized
- powerless
- oppressed

1. Roy E. Ciampa, "The History of Redemption," in *Central Themes of Biblical Theology: Mapping Unity in Diversity*, ed. Scott J. Hafemann and Paul R. House (Grand Rapids: Baker, 2007), 292n94.

- dependent upon God
- humble
- righteous
- exiled

The identity of the poor as the people of God in James is additionally clarified by the identity of the rich. In this letter, the rich are not merely those who have many possessions, but those who are proud (1:9–11), heading for an eschatological humiliation (1:9–11), oppressors, defrauders, persecutors of believers (2:5–7; 5:1–6), blasphemers of Christ (2:7), and ultimately those who are severely punished by God, who avenges his people (5:1–6).[2]

As we determined when considering the context of James, four distinct groups appear to be referenced in the epistle: (1) the poor (the majority in this believing community), (2) the severely poor (2:14–17; those without decent clothes and often in need of daily food), (3) merchants (4:13–16; those who were tempted to be overconfident in their ability to buy, sell, and make a profit), and (4) wealthy landowners (1:9–11; 5:1–6; those who were exploiting and persecuting the poor in the believing community). The congregations were composed of the first three groups, with the majority being in the first group, which might best be characterized as the working people of the land. This group comprised the majority in these churches, as well as the vast majority of the regional population. In the first century, many worked as tenants on large estates, while others were day laborers, hoping to find good work and often finding it only around harvest.

In this particular historical and Jewish context, James stresses that the poor are cared for by God (cf. Deut. 10:18; Ps. 68:5) and deserve protection by God's people (cf. Deut. 10:19).[3]

2. Duane Warden, "The Rich and Poor in James: Implications for Institutionalized Partiality," *Journal of the Evangelical Society* 43, no. 2 (June 2000): 247–57.

3. Forgetful of this context is liberation theology, which tends to reduce Christianity to the defense of the oppressed.

Kamell reminds us that throughout the Old Testament, the treatment of the poor is directly tied to concepts of justice (Ex. 23:6; Lev. 19:15; Deut. 27:19; Isa. 11:4; Jer. 7:8–10).[4] Likewise, McCartney observes:

> The notion of the community of faith being the poor has its roots in the Old Testament (cf. Ps. 86:1 where it is the poor who are deeply aware that they are dependent on God). The Qumran community also regarded itself as the community of the poor (1QH 2:5, 1QpHab 12:3, 6, 10, 4QpPs37 2:9; 3:10). It is precisely because the community is the poor that they deserve respect (James 2:1–7) and why dishonoring them is so contrary to true faith (2:6, an echo of Prov. 14:31, which declares dishonoring the poor man to be an insult to his Maker).[5]

James also reflects the teaching of Jesus, who frequently denounced the exploitive rich and defended the oppressed poor. Parallels with Jesus' teaching here are remarkable: blessing the poor and warning the rich (James 1:9–10; Luke 6:20–24), the poor as recipients of the kingdom (James 2:5; Matt. 5:3; Luke 6:20), the poor being spiritually rich (James 2:5; Luke 12:21), mercy given to the merciful (James 2:13; Matt. 5:7; 18:21–35), final salvation evidenced in feeding and clothing fellow believers (James 2:14–17; Matt. 25:34–46), the transitory nature of life (James 4:13–16; Matt. 6:34), judgment coming on the rich (James 5:1–6: Luke 6:24–25), and the vulnerability of stored-up wealth to moths and corrosion (James 5:2–4; Matt. 6:19–20).

James's theme of poverty is also related to other challenges facing the churches: trials, favoritism, faith and works, conflicts, presumption, exploitation, and patience. Because of this, James addresses the issue in several passages, and from them we find several insights.

4. Mariam Kamell, "The Economics of Humility: The Rich and the Humble in James," in *Economic Dimensions of Early Christianity*, ed. Bruce Longenecker and Kelly Leibengood (Grand Rapids: Eerdmans, 2009), 163.

5. Dan G. McCartney, "Suffering and the Apostles," in *Suffering and the Goodness of God*, ed. Christopher W. Morgan and Robert A. Peterson, Theology in Community (Wheaton, IL: Crossway, 2008), 104.

- The Righteous Poor Find Hope in a Future Reversal (1:9–11).
- God's People Must Care for the Poor (1:26–27).
- God Has Chosen the Poor to Inherit the Kingdom (2:1–13).
- God's People Should Not Discriminate against the Poor (2:1–13).
- Genuine Faith Demonstrates Itself in Works of Love for the Poor (2:14–17).
- Presumption Regarding Life and Wealth Displays Pride (4:13–17).
- God Hears the Cries of the Righteous Poor and Will Vindicate Them (5:1–6).

The Righteous Poor Find Hope in a Future Reversal (1:9-11)

James 1:9–11 teaches poverty-stricken believers that being righteous and exploited is far better than being the wicked exploiters. In this passage, James introduces a theme woven throughout Scripture and especially emphasized by Jesus: eschatological reversal (cf. Luke 6:20–26; 16:19–31; 18:18–30). The "lowly" believer should "boast in his exaltation" (1:9). The lowly believer sits at the bottom of the pecking order—poor, undistinguished in position, power, and esteem. But the humble brother is actually exalted—exalted in Christ. He does have something to boast about: his present and future exaltation and blessedness.

But the rich should boast in their humiliation (1:10). Perhaps James alludes to the saying of Jesus recorded in Luke 14:11: "For everyone who exalts himself will be humbled, and he who humbles himself will be exalted." Some interpreters question whether "the rich" in 1:10 include believers. Although it is linguistically possible, it is unnecessary because the word "brother" (used for the poor in verse 9) is not repeated. And theologically, it is much wiser to interpret the rich as unbelievers because their fate is destruction and ruin. James's statements about the rich and the poor throughout also assume the Old Testament literary usage: the poor are righteous, and the rich are oppressive (cf. Luke 12:13–21; 16:19–31).

The destiny of the rich is further spelled out in 1:10–11. The rich (not just their riches) pass away like dried-up wild flowers on a scorching hot day. Indeed, the rich man will "fade away in the midst of his pursuits" (1:11). Kamell encapsulates what James is saying:

> Ultimately, humility or humiliation will come to every person, whether rich or poor; the question is whether one chooses to humble oneself (James 4:10) or be humbled (1:10); and how one treats the desperately poor is a key indication of each person's status as humble or not before the Lord. The truly humble will practice the economics of humility in caring for the helpless rather than flaunting their wealth as their own possession and right.[6]

God's People Must Care for the Poor (1:26–27)

This passage is central to James. This is clear, not only because of its structural implications for the book, but also because of how many themes are linked to it—consistency, suffering, words, love and mercy, and the poor. Among other things, it makes plain that God's people have a special responsibility to care for the poor and oppressed. This is not merely the mark of spiritual elites, but of what James calls "pure and undefiled religion before God."

Scripture instructs us to worship corporately, to listen to the reading, teaching, and preaching of Scripture, to give, to pray, to participate in the Lord's Supper, etc. These are important spiritual activities that God has prescribed for us as we follow him. But James warns that too often people think that participation in the outward expressions of religion is all that God demands. James stresses that the practice of religion occurs not merely in worship services, but also in how we live our lives. God wants worship through consistent lives. And part of this way of life includes showing love to those

6. Kamell, "The Economics of Humility," 175.

whom God loves—the poor and oppressed. Ben Witherington notes, "Our discourse is about a God who is impartial, faithful, righteous, just, merciful—and who requires of his followers the same sort of behavior."[7] Daniel Doriani puts it penetratingly: "Kindness to the needy is God-like. *We* sustain aliens, widows, and orphans because *he* sustains aliens, widows, and orphans (Ps. 146:9)."[8] True religion, that which pleases God, means that we reflect God by actively ministering to the poor and oppressed.

James 1:26–27 forcefully contrasts two different approaches to religion, both of which must have been vying for people's allegiance. True religion is "pure," undefiled," and accepted by God. It is concerned with verbal self-control, active love for the poor, and moral purity. Some undercurrents are at play here. James calls true religion "pure and undefiled," and thereby implies that the religion embraced by some is impure and defiled. Their so-called worship is unclean, contaminated, and unsuitable for the holy God. James refers to true religion as keeping oneself "unstained from the world" (1:27), implying that some are preoccupied with ritual cleanness without corresponding interest in moral cleanness or godly values. And by stressing that God accepts true religion, he implies that God rejects other approaches. That James calls other efforts at worship "worthless" (1:26) strengthens that effect. Any other religion is worthless because it does not demonstrate love for God or love for others. Indeed, it is worthless because it does not demonstrate love for God *through* loving others.

Martin Luther, not known for his affection for James, frequently stressed this very point. Luther complained that believers should not live in monasteries to serve God, because there they were actually only serving themselves. Instead, Christians must follow Christ and love and serve their neighbors through their vocations in the world, where their neighbors encounter and need them. Luther argued, "God does not need our good

7. Ben Witherington III, *Letters and Homilies for Jewish Christians: A Socio-Rhetorical Commentary on Hebrews, James and Jude* (Downers Grove, IL: InterVarsity Press, 2007), 436.

8. Daniel M. Doriani, *James*, Reformed Expository Commentary (Phillipsburg, NJ: P&R Publishing, 2007), 59 (emphasis in original).

works, but our neighbor does."[9] When we seek to offer our good works to God, we actually display pride before God and neglect to love our neighbor. Luther contends that in so doing we parade ourselves before God and yet fail to do the very thing that Jesus commands. In other words, we fail both to love God and to love others. Michael Horton ably captures Luther's point:

> God descends to serve humanity through our vocations, so instead of seeing good works as our works for God, they are now to be seen as God's work for our neighbor, which God performs through us. That is why both orders are upset when we seek to present good works to God as if he needed them. In contrast, when we are overwhelmed by the superabundance of God's gracious gift, we express our gratitude in horizontal works of love and service to the neighbor.[10]

Love is not self-absorbed, but genuinely seeks the welfare of others. It is active and outward. Luther is right: religious people often feel noble when they perform external religious acts, believing that they are serving God. But as Solomon Andria suggests, "Rather than serving God, they serve themselves."[11]

Serving others feels far less noble; it often seems only mundane, even insignificant. Yet Jesus washed his disciples' feet and demands that his followers do the same. Jesus' command would not be so burdensome if he merely required that we wash his feet; we could find dignity in helping Jesus. But Jesus demands that we wash one another's feet, which reduces us to feeling like unimportant, humble servants. And that is exactly what James stresses: genuine, humble, dependent, loving followers of Jesus will display their true concern for others through ministering to others, particularly those with desperate needs.

Some in James's audience were more concerned about ritual purity than moral purity, and they were content to express empty

9. Gustav Wingren, *Luther on Vocation*, trans. Carl C. Rasmussen (Philadelphia: Muhlenberg Press, 1957; reprint, Evansville, IN: Ballast Press, 2004), 2.

10. Michael S. Horton, *People and Place: A Covenant Ecclesiology* (Louisville, KY: Westminster John Knox, 2008), 304.

11. Solomon Andria, "James," in *Africa Bible Commentary*, ed. Tokunboh Adeyemo (Grand Rapids: Zondervan, 2006), 1514.

words without showing active compassion for the oppressed. Ironically, some in these congregations stressed the ritual purity taught in Leviticus, but failed to notice that Leviticus also stresses moral purity and especially love for the oppressed. It is not by coincidence that James refers frequently to Leviticus 19 as a basis of his instructions. He takes his audience back to study the very law they claim to be defending.

To such people, James says that true religion is "to visit orphans and widows in their affliction" (1:27), and thus reiterates the teachings of Exodus 22:22 ("You shall not mistreat any widow or fatherless child") and Isaiah 1:17 ("Bring justice to the fatherless, plead the widow's cause"). Elsewhere, the Old Testament often makes plain these requirements for acceptable religion and worship (cf. Deut. 10:16–19; Ps. 69:32–33; Zech. 7:9–14). Together, widows and orphans represented those who were without protection or provision. There was no government assistance in those days, so the loss of a husband or parents was often financially devastating. Consistent with the teaching of the Old Testament and the practice of the earliest church (cf. Acts 2:42–47; 4:32–37; 5:1–11; 6:1–7; 11:19–30), James instructs the church to assume responsibility for the support of the poor, the disadvantaged, and the oppressed.[12] In so doing, he again reflects the teachings of Jesus, who declared that one's treatment of "the least of these" is linked to future judgment (Matt. 25:31–46).

God Has Chosen the Poor to Inherit the Kingdom (2:1–13)

To understand God's choice of the poor to inherit the kingdom, it is important to keep in mind James's usage of the terms "poor" and "rich." James is not saying that God has elected all

12. Dan McCartney's words bear repeating: "The church is the community that anticipates the eschatological reversal by caring for and respecting the poor. . . . Partiality belies the eschatological nature of the community, which ought to display in advance God's exaltation of the poor." McCartney, "Suffering and the Apostles," 107; cf. Craig L. Blomberg, *Neither Poverty nor Riches: A Biblical Theology of Possessions*, New Studies in Biblical Theology (Downers Grove, IL: InterVarsity Press, 1999).

poor people for salvation. Many poor persons reject Christ and are quite obviously not rich in faith or heirs of the kingdom. James speaks of the "poor" in the same way that Jesus and the Old Testament do, referring to the humble and the righteous poor, the people of God who are disadvantaged, oppressed, or destitute. Jesus teaches, "Blessed are you who are poor" and includes them in his kingdom (Luke 6:20). Indeed, his preaching to, and inclusion of, the poor was linked to his identity and mission as the Messiah (Luke 4:18–20; Isa. 61:1–2).

God's choice of the poor here is for salvation. He chose them "to be rich in faith and heirs of the kingdom, which he has promised to those who love him" (James 2:5). Election here is a broad term, but it is for faith and for salvation in the kingdom, linked to the promise of God, and tied only to those who love him. God's election is gracious and initiating. It results in faith in Christ, love for God, and kingdom citizenship. The poor are not chosen simply because of their financial condition, just as the rich are not rejected because of their wealth. But the poor often recognize that they need God, while the rich are often self-satisfied and proud (cf. 1 Cor. 1:18–31). James reminds those who idealize the rich that the poor are graciously included in the people of God.

James 2:1–13 relates some wonderful truths about these righteous poor. First, although rejected by the world, they are chosen by God. Second, despite being poor in worldly possessions, they are rich in faith. Third, they are heirs of God's kingdom. Fourth, they are therefore recipients of the promise. Finally, they love God. Using these characterizations, James shows that the righteous poor are eternally blessed.

God's People Should Not Discriminate against the Poor (2:1-13)

James 1:26–27 addresses true religion, and 2:1 begins with the same line of thought, though utilizing different terminology.

True religion consists of more than conformity to a set of outward standards—it is genuine faith, faith in the Lord of glory, expressing itself in righteous behavior. Such faith in Jesus, James argues, is inconsistent with partiality against the poor.

James 2:2–3 pictures two newcomers entering the church, here called the "assembly" (in Greek, literally, "synagogue"). One man is wealthy, finely dressed and wearing a gold ring. In sharp contrast, the other man is poor and wearing shabby clothes. Those greeting the well-dressed man give him the red-carpet treatment, and even invite him to occupy a seat of honor (cf. Matt. 23:6). The poor person, on the other hand, is treated with disdain and is told to stand off to the side or sit by someone's feet.

James points out the inconsistency by asking a rhetorical question (2:4), accusing these church members of partiality as well as judging with evil thoughts. James essentially asserts, "You say you believe in the Lord Jesus, don't you? Then, follow his example and teaching about loving others, especially the hurting and the poor." He then recalls God's love for the poor, which we previously discussed.

James rebukes those who show partiality further in 2:6–7 and then asks two questions to expose their sin. His rebuke is pointed: "You have dishonored the poor man" (2:6). To discriminate against people on the basis of social status or wealth disgraces those to whom God has granted grace; it rejects those whom God accepts. This is judging with evil thoughts (2:4). "You" is emphatic, and the word translated "have dishonored" means more than to ignore; it is the idea of shaming someone—a strong statement in a culture that values honor. James is upset because those who say they are followers of Jesus are shaming the very people whom Jesus includes (cf. Luke 14–16).

James then asks three questions, each expecting a positive answer, and thus declaring the foolishness of those showing partiality. Note the incongruity of each. (1) Godless, affluent people exploit the Christians who court their favor. (2) Those given the best seats return the favor by dragging Christians into court. (3) Those whom these people favor blaspheme the honorable name of Jesus. James asserts that to dishonor the poor is to dishonor Jesus' name and thus to dishonor Jesus himself.

Andrew Chester comments on James's understanding of the rich and how people treat them:

> James, in these sections, exposes ruthlessly the sources of power, the nature of power relationships and the causes of conflict, oppression, and social injustice. To live for personal gain and to exploit the poor and defenceless is the epitome of evil, above all because it is set in direct contradiction to what God requires (2:5). Yet at the same time James insists that it is not simply the direct exploitation and oppression of the poor by the rich that constitutes the problem. It is also the obsequious favouring of the rich and powerful, for the favour it is hoped they will bestow, and the contemptuous treatment of the poor, because they can offer nothing, that serves to reinforce the injustice, suffering and imbalance of power.[13]

The people of God are to honor and show mercy to the poor. James 2:8–13 develops this theme and moves from the particular example of discrimination to the broader teaching of Scripture. James points his readers back to the law, especially drawing attention to Leviticus 19, the teachings of Jesus (Matt. 22:37–40), and the Ten Commandments (Ex. 20). He reminds the congregations of a fundamental command: "You shall love your neighbor as yourself" (2:8; cf. Lev. 19:18). Leviticus 19—which makes provisions for honoring and showing love to the poor, oppressed, deaf, blind, sojourners, servants, women, and elderly—mandates compassion for everyone, not just for those the world values. Discriminating against the poor thus blatantly contradicts the law and is sinful (2:9). And because the law is a unity, James's readers need to remember that even if they meticulously keep the law in all other points, yet fail in the royal law of love, they transgress and stumble in all its points (2:9–11). To transgress any part of the divine law exposes

13. Andrew Chester and Ralph P. Martin, *The Theology of the Letters of James, Peter, and Jude*, New Testament Theology (New York: Cambridge University Press, 1996), 33.

a lack of covenant faithfulness and violates both the whole law and the Lawgiver (cf. Gal. 3:10).

James details how this works by referencing two of the Ten Commandments, the prohibitions of adultery and murder. He also draws attention to the personal nature of the law. "He who said" (2:11) reminds the reader that this is God's law, and that it has authority because of the One who uttered it; the law is the covenant Lord and Lawgiver speaking (cf. 4:11–12). James likely intends us to understand this prohibition of murder in light of Jesus' interpretation (e.g., applying it to the murderous and hateful heart in Matthew 5:21–26). One who avoids adultery but commits murder, whether literally or as a wrong spiritual attitude, is nevertheless a lawbreaker. James personalizes his argument here by ushering us to the future judgment: "So speak and so act as those who are to be judged under the law of liberty. For judgment is without mercy to one who has shown no mercy. Mercy triumphs over judgment" (2:12–13; cf. Matt. 18:21–35). In essence, he warns the covenant communities: "Discrimination against the poor is not only absurd, but serious. To fail to love and show mercy to the poor is to be guilty as a lawbreaker." But James the pastor also promotes the people's welfare by pointing to their possible repentance. Yes, judgment is without mercy to those who show no mercy, but it is also true that mercy triumphs over judgment. In other words, James urges, "Show mercy. Repent and love the poor as God does and as his law commands." Indeed, "Blessed are the merciful, for they shall receive mercy" (Matt. 5:7).

Genuine Faith Demonstrates Itself in Works of Love for the Poor (2:14–17)

God's people should not only not discriminate against the poor, but also show love to them. In 2:14–17, James teaches that the good works evidencing salvation include more than prayers and benedictions. True faith leads to love for, and ministry to, the poor.

When James gives instructions about the necessity of faith and good works, he chooses as his first example the need to help the poor (2:14–26). Indeed, the previous discussion related to the mistreatment of the poor gives rise both to his discussion of the law of liberty (2:8–13) and to his famous teaching about faith and works (2:14–26).

The messages of James 1:26–27, 2:1–13, and 2:14–17 are similar. James 1:26–27 teaches that true and undefiled religion includes ministering to the widow and the orphan. James 2:1–13 makes plain that faith in Jesus, divine election, the law, and the prospect of judgment require loving the poor and prohibit discrimination against them. Here in James 2:14–17 we find that faith has works, and particularly works of love for the poor.

The argument is straightforward. James pointedly asks two questions: "What good is it, my brothers, if someone says he has faith but does not have works? Can that faith save him?" (2:14). James highlights the utter uselessness of such so-called faith. Faith without works is useless because it does not justify the supposed believer and because it does not help the needy.

James illustrates this in 2:15–16, again with regard to the treatment of the poor. He paints a scene where fellow believers in need of basic necessities, such as food and clothes, come into contact with the church.[14] Instead of getting actual help from a loving Christian community, the poor receive only a farewell blessing: "Go in peace, be warmed and filled" (2:16). "Go in peace" was a common Jewish farewell—shalom (cf. Judges 18:6; 1 Sam. 1:17; 20:42; 2 Sam. 15:9). Today it would be like saying, "Good-bye and God bless you." Instead of the poor receiving warm clothes and satisfying food, all they get is religious triteness. Their words speak of grace, but they fail to minister grace. How can they go in peace, when they will be hungry and cold? And how do the professing Christians expect God to bless these needy people? Would it not be natural to think that God intends to bless the poor through his covenant people? Even more, how can these professing Christians

---

14. Kamell ("The Economics of Humility," 165) observes that James uses the same two illustrations as Deuteronomy 10:18.

claim to follow Christ while loving their possessions more than the needy? Jonathan Edwards maintained, "To love our neighbor as ourselves is the sum of the moral law respecting our fellow-creatures; and to help them, and to contribute to their relief, is the most natural expression of this love. It is vain to pretend to a spirit of love to our neighbors, when it is grievous to us to part with any thing for their help."[15]

This illustration uncovers the hypocrisy of faith apart from works, of religion apart from love for the poor. So James makes his point: "So also faith by itself, if it does not have works, is dead" (2:17).

Presumption Regarding Life and Wealth Displays Pride (4:13-17)

James addresses the moderately wealthy in his warning that those in business should be careful to live in utter dependence on God and not presume that they have the ability to succeed financially on their own. In a story that resembles Jesus' parable about the rich fool (Luke 12:16–21), James imagines some of the businessmen from the churches sitting around their conference tables, making plans for future ventures (4:13). They exude confidence, to say the least. They speak without restraint of what they will do, where they will go, and what profit they will make. They assume their ability to forecast and accomplish their plans. But they are wrong, and James underscores their pride and presumption.

It is important to clarify that planning is good, wise, and necessary. We should not interpret this verse as a denunciation of planning for the future. The problem is not the planning, but the arrogance and presumption reflected in their words. The four verbs are all future: "will go," "will spend a year," "will trade," and "will make a profit." The verse reveals five areas of arrogant

---

15. Jonathan Edwards, "Christian Charity: Duty of Charity to the Poor, Explained and Enforced," in *The Works of Jonathan Edwards*, ed. Edward Hickman, 2 vols. (Edinburgh: Banner of Truth Trust, 1974), 2:165.

90

certainty about their plans: certainty of the future (we will go), of place (into "this or that" city), of time (spend a year), of activity (trade), and of result (make a profit).[16]

This attitude toward life and money is foolish, because such presumption forgets that we do not know what the future holds and cannot control it (only the sovereign God does), and our lives are short. James here echoes the teaching of Proverbs, "Do not boast about tomorrow, for you do not know what a day may bring forth" (Prov. 27:1). His message also recalls Jesus' words in the Sermon on the Mount:

> Therefore I tell you, do not be anxious about your life, what you will eat or what you will drink, nor about your body, what you will put on. Is not life more than food, and the body more than clothing? Look at the birds of the air: they neither sow nor reap nor gather into barns, and yet your heavenly Father feeds them. Are you not of more value than they? And which of you by being anxious can add a single hour to his span of life? And why are you anxious about clothing? Consider the lilies of the field, how they grow: they neither toil nor spin, yet I tell you, even Solomon in all his glory was not arrayed like one of these. But if God so clothes the grass of the field, which today is alive and tomorrow is thrown into the oven, will he not much more clothe you, O you of little faith? Therefore do not be anxious, saying, "What shall we eat?" or "What shall we drink?" or "What shall we wear?" For the Gentiles seek after all these things, and your heavenly Father knows that you need them all. But seek first the kingdom of God and his righteousness, and all these things will be added to you. Therefore do not be anxious about tomorrow, for tomorrow will be anxious for itself. Sufficient for the day is its own trouble. (Matt. 6:25–34)

James continues, reminding these merchants that life is short (4:14). The word translated "mist" could refer to mist that rolls in from the sea and then vanishes, which would be especially

16. See Christopher W. Morgan and B. Dale Ellenburg, *James: Wisdom for the Community* (Fearn, UK: Christian Focus Publications, 2008), 159–66.

picturesque for sea merchants. Then in 4:15 James directs, "Instead you ought to say, 'If the Lord wills, we will live and do this or that.'" He contrasts the arrogant "you who say" (4:13) with the humbler "you ought to say" (4:15). Instead of speaking out of pride and presumption, the merchants should express themselves in a way that displays their submission to God and his sovereignty (cf. Acts 18:21; 1 Cor. 4:19; 16:7; Phil. 2:19, 24; Heb. 6:3). James 4:16 states their error: they boast in their arrogance. He then adds: "All such boasting is evil. So whoever knows the right thing to do and fails to do it, for him it is sin" (4:16–17).

God Hears the Cries of the Righteous Poor and Will Vindicate Them (5:1–6)

Justice comes now only occasionally, but ultimately it will prevail. Like an Old Testament prophet, James castigates the rich who have exploited the poor. The oppressors should weep and wail because God's judgment on them will be severe. Misery and suffering are coming their way. The corrosion of their wealth will serve as a witness against them, and the wages they failed to pay their workers will testify against them. By living in luxury and self-indulgence, they increase their punishment at the last judgment. In light of the coming judgment, the righteous poor are to be patient and not grumble against each other, knowing that they too will be judged (5:7–11).

This passage powerfully reveals James's theology of the poor and the rich. It puts forward three truths: (1) God hears the cries of the righteous poor. (2) God will punish those who oppress the righteous poor. (3) God will vindicate the righteous poor by punishing the wicked and blessing the righteous who endure. Let's look at each in turn.

James graphically proclaims, "Behold, the wages of the laborers who mowed your fields, which you kept back by fraud, are crying out against you, and the cries of the harvesters have reached the ears of the Lord of hosts" (5:4). James states that the stolen money and the laborers themselves will loudly cry out against these oppressive rich people at the judgment. Evidently, the wages of hired laborers were being dishonestly withheld by rich landowners. These day laborers mowed and harvested the fields of absentee landlords. Their earnings were paltry, and they were to be paid every day because they could not afford to miss a paycheck. These defenseless workers toiled daily under a blistering sun only to be swindled by rich, powerful landowners. The landowners methodically held back their wages, defrauding their powerless employees. Alec Motyer reminds us that the practice of paying wages late or defrauding the worker of his wage was not unusual. That is why many Old Testament laws and prophetic threats declare God's hatred of the practice (Lev. 19:13; Deut. 24:14–15; Jer. 22:13; Mal. 3:5).[17] James dramatically portrays the withheld wages' shrieking cry, followed by the cry of the harvesters themselves. But who hears this cry? The wicked landowners certainly do not; they are enjoying luxurious lives, too self-indulgent to care (5:5).[18] The corrupt justice system does not hear their cry, for it curries the favor of the wealthy. Is anyone with power to help listening to these cries? Oh, yes! God himself, the omnipotent Lord of hosts, hears these cries (5:4).

When God's people utter cries in the Bible, they are usually praying for deliverance from danger and seeking justice (cf. Ex. 2:23; 1 Sam. 9:16; 2 Chron. 33:13).[19] Johnson observes, "Here James definitely evokes the experience of Israel in Egypt. At the burning bush Yahweh says to Moses, 'I have seen the affliction of my people in Egypt and I have heard their shouts' (Exod. 3:7)."[20]

Here too the cries of the exploited poor "have reached" the Lord of hosts (5:4). This depiction of God as "the Lord of hosts," or "the Lord of armies," is frequent in the Old Testament, where

17. J. A. Motyer, *The Message of James*, Bible Speaks Today (Downers Grove, IL: InterVarsity Press, 1985), 177. James's teaching again reflects Leviticus 19.

18. Other sins related to money in this passage include greed, hoarding wealth, defrauding others, living in excessive luxury, and self-indulgence.

19. Douglas J. Moo, *The Letter of James*, Pillar New Testament Commentary (Grand Rapids: Eerdmans, 2000), 54.

20. Luke Timothy Johnson, *The Letter of James*, The Anchor Bible (New York: Doubleday, 1995), 302.

God is likened to a warrior leading an army of warriors who slay enemies and enforce justice. The Lord of all power will come to the aid of the suffering, not only hearing the cries of the righteous poor, but also punishing their oppressors and bringing vindication. As in James 1:9–11, a grand and final reversal will take place at the final judgment.

Plainly, insightful teaching related to the poor abounds in James. But James is not content if only good theology abounds. Love for and ministry to the poor must abound as well. Like Micah 6:8, James urges God's people to be characterized by justice, mercy, and humility.[21]

21. Kamell, "The Economics of Humility," 166.

8

Words

JAMES'S THEME of speech, addressed in all five chapters of the epistle, expresses his pastoral burden for wisdom for consistency in the community. Believers' appropriate use of words displays covenant faithfulness, whereas inappropriate words display pride and hypocrisy. Pastors know the significance of church members' use of words, and all pastors have watched the blessings and curses that result. The believing communities addressed by James were having problems in this area, so he tackles the issues head-on and exhorts them concerning their speech. Wiard Popkes wittily characterizes the churches to which James writes as churches of the word— and of words![1]

- Words Must Come Slowly, Especially Angry Ones (1:19–21).
- Controlled Words Follow True Faith (1:26; 2:14–17).
- Words Must Be Spoken with the Judgment in View (2:12).
- Words Must Not Be a Substitute for Action (2:14–17).
- Words Are Powerful and Can Hurt the Church (3:1–12).
- Words Reflect the Heart and Thus Manifest Consistency or Double-mindedness (3:9–12).

1. Wiard Popkes, *Adressaten, Situation und Form des Jakobusbriefes* (Stuttgart: Katholische Bibelwerk, 1986), 103. I owe this reference to I. H. Marshall, *New Testament Theology: Many Witnesses, One Gospel* (Downers Grove, IL: InterVarsity Press, 2004), 639.

- Words of Slander Are Sinful and Will Be Judged (4:11–12; 5:9).
- Words Must Display Submission to God, Not Pride or Boasting (4:13–17).
- Truthful Words Must Characterize God's People (5:12).
- Words Must Edify the Church (5:13–20).

Words Must Come Slowly, Especially Angry Ones (1:19–21)

Memorably, James urges the churches, "Let every person be quick to hear, slow to speak, slow to anger" (1:19). Before and after this, James gives attention to the word of God. He explains that we were brought forth into a new creation through it (1:18), that we need to receive it with meekness (1:21), and that we need to hear and practice it (1:22–25). James is not telling people to talk less and listen more, but urging the churches to listen to God's word and be slow to use angry words. Angry words do not lead to God's righteousness, but to damaged relationships and weakened churches.

Yet again James strikes the chord of both the Old Testament and Jesus. Proverbs often treats this matter and puts it simply, "Whoever restrains his words has knowledge" (17:27). Jesus reveals that sinful anger is forbidden in his kingdom: "You have heard that it was said to those of old, 'You shall not murder; and whoever murders will be liable to judgment.' But I say to you that everyone who is angry with his brother will be liable to judgment; whoever insults his brother will be liable to the council; and whoever says, 'You fool!' will be liable to the hell of fire" (Matt. 5:21–22).

Being slow to anger does not mean never getting angry. On the contrary, God is angry at sin and sinners (Rom. 1:18–32); Jesus expressed righteous indignation against sin (Mark 3:5). Godly anger is focused on sin and controlled in its expressions; ungodly anger, however, is linked to human pride and self-will. It should be considered sin and dealt with quickly (Matt. 5:23–25; Eph.

4:26) because it does not produce righteousness, but all sorts of evil, particularly in churches. Such anger and its corresponding hateful speech require repentance, not patience. James insists that his readers rid themselves of angry words and receive God's word (1:21).[2]

Controlled Words Follow True Faith (1:26; 2:14-17)

In James's explanation of the distinctives of genuine religion (1:26–27), the control of the tongue is first on the list. True faith leads people to control their tongues, James stresses. Those who do not do so only deceive themselves (1:26).

James restates this idea in 2:14–17. Robert Wall captures James's point as well as the relationship between 1:26–27 and 2:14–17:

> The importance of this particular contrast between empty speech and active compassion is developed later in this section, when James contrasts spoken and enacted faith (2:14–26). In this case, believers who profess their faith (v. 14) but dismiss the poor (v. 15), even with sincere benediction (v. 16), fail to meet God's eschatological requirement of merciful work (v. 17, cf. v. 13). . . . In wider compositional context, then, the "tongue" that "says" the slogans of pious religion as though that is all that God requires is deceived and therefore unable to pass the testing of faith. . . .
>
> Coupled with the phrase "bridling the tongue," a "worthless" religion is one in which what is said replaces what is done, where talk is substituted for walk, where liturgy rather than lifestyle expresses the community's devotion to God. But in what sense is this species of religion "worthless"? Clearly, this species of religion fails to receive God's blessing simply because it fails to bear witness to God by deed and is therefore

2. Recall 1 Peter 2:1–2, "So put away all malice and all deceit and hypocrisy and envy and all slander. Like newborn infants, long for the pure spiritual milk, that by it you may grow up to salvation," and Psalm 119:11, "I have stored up your word in my heart, that I might not sin against you."

worthless. More importantly, however, this religion contributes no social benefaction; it is also worthless to the poor who constitute God's people (2:5).[3]

True faith and love evidence themselves in actions, and that includes controlling our words.

Words Must Be Spoken with the Judgment in View (2:12)

James 2:8–13, which we will examine in more detail in the chapter "God's Word and Law," warns that we must speak and act in light of the coming judgment (2:8–13). More simply, we will be judged by our words and our works. This is reminiscent of Jesus' proclamation in Matthew 12:36–37, "I tell you, on the day of judgment people will give account for every careless word they speak, for by your words you will be justified, and by your words you will be condemned."

Words Must Not Be a Substitute for Action (2:14–17)

The principle that words are not a substitute for action has been addressed and is straightforward enough. When people need clothes, simply giving them your blessing leaves them as they came—inadequately covered. When people are hungry, wishing them well still leaves them hungry. As Solomon Andria puts it, "Fine-sounding words would not feed them, nor would good wishes."[4]

Like good works, good words flow from a heart that loves God and others and wants to help them. Blessings and benedictions are good, but good words that are devoid of corresponding good works reveal duplicity rather than a genuine heart that

---

3. Robert W. Wall, *Community of the Wise: The Letter of James*, New Testament in Context (Valley Forge, PA: Trinity Press International, 1997), 99–100.

4. Solomon Andria, "James," in *Africa Bible Commentary*, ed. Tokunboh Adeyemo (Grand Rapids: Zondervan, 2006), 1514.

loves to help others. Just as faith without works is dead, so words without works are dead, empty, and useless, displaying a double-minded heart.

Words Are Powerful and Can Hurt the Church (3:1–12)

In some instances, our words are problematic because they are not linked to helpful actions. Such words lack power and are sins of omission—failure to do what is right. At other times, however, words are sinful because they communicate evil, such as hatred and bitterness. In this text, words exert much power and are expressions of sins of commission—actions that are wrong. James again follows the Old Testament wisdom tradition, which castigates rumors, gossip, and slander. Such failure to control one's words often damages community (Prov. 16:28; 26:20).[5]

James 3:1–12 begins by emphasizing that not many should presume themselves to be teachers, because teachers will receive a stricter judgment (3:1). And we find in 3:13–18 that some in these churches supposed themselves to be spiritually wise and worthy of the role. James questions their assumptions about their spirituality and raises the standards for being a teacher.

We do not know how formal the teaching role was at this early stage in the church. Teachers likely functioned in Christian churches much like they did in Jewish synagogues. In Jewish life at that time, it was prestigious for a family to have a son training to be a rabbi, and so it is likely that Jewish Christians would tend to give the same respect to Christian teachers.[6] In time, the pastor-teacher would become more formal and arguably an office (cf. Eph. 4:11). In first-century synagogues and churches, teachers were very influential and prominent. Sometimes such a role draws those who want influence and prominence, rather than those who want to serve others.

5. Tremper Longman III, *Proverbs*, Baker Commentary on the Old Testament (Grand Rapids: Baker, 2006), 568–69.

6. Larry L. Walker, "Speech and Wisdom (James 3)," *Mid-America Theological Journal* 10, no. 1 (Spring 1986): 43.

James hopes to help the churches by exposing unqualified candidates and highlighting the gravity of being a teacher. Would-be teachers should not presume themselves to be worthy, but take seriously the weighty responsibility of the role and the stricter judgment it incurs. Tidball reminds us:

> John Chrysostom (347–407) became one of the outstanding pastors of the early church, but he initially resisted the invitation to become a bishop. When asked why he was so reluctant, he argued, with irresistible logic, that no one would consider pulling any old person out of the crowd, turning them into a military dignitary and insisting they head up a great army. It would be stupid. Turning to another illustration, he said they would be foolish to entrust a fully-laden merchant ship into the hands of an inexperienced sea captain like himself, lest I should sink the ship. But in that case, as he points out, the only loss would be a material one. In the church, by contrast, the loss caused by inept or inexperienced handling of people will be eternal. No wonder James writes, "Not many of you should become teachers."[7]

James holds the standard high (indeed, at perfection in 3:2b), but concedes that "we all stumble in many ways" (3:2a). James is quick to admit that all of us sin, himself included (note the use of "we"), but also reminds us of the seriousness of controlling our words. To do so, he uses six illustrations: a bit (3:3), a rudder (3:4), a fire (3:5–6), a poisonous animal (3:7–8), a spring (3:11), and a fig tree (3:12). Reiterating 1:26, James urges us to bridle our lives, and our tongues in particular (3:2). Even if no one controls his words flawlessly, mature people do exhibit overall control of them (3:2). James then gives two examples of how something small can exert influence seemingly out of proportion to its size: bits for horses (3:3) and rudders for ships (3:4). The tongue is

---

7. Derek Tidball, *Wisdom from Heaven: The Message of the Letter of James for Today* (Fearn, UK: Christian Focus Publications, 2003), 102. Tidball refers to John Chrysostom, *On the Priesthood*, Nicene and Post-Nicene Fathers (repr., Grand Rapids: Eerdmans, 1978–79), 3.7.49.

likened to both the bit and the rudder in that it is a small thing, yet sizable in its influence (3:5). The neutral examples give way to negative ones in 3:6–7. The tongue is compared to a destructive fire, a defiler of the whole body,[8] and a world of unrighteousness. Using these images, James warns that the tongue has influence, and that too often it produces contamination and destruction, rather than blessing and edification. He seems to have the church in view when he uses the word "body." Ralph Martin concurs: "The implication is that by irresponsible speech the whole body of Christ is stained."[9]

James urges the churches to watch out for those who use their words to slander others. Those biting words are more destructive than they first appear and more pervasive than anyone would suppose. Plus, their source is more troubling than people would like to admit; the tongue is "set on fire by hell" (3:6). James Motyer states it well: "The first feature of the tongue was that it was anti-God (the world); the last feature is that it is pro-Satan."[10] Underlining the danger of proud and hypocritical words, James exclaims that the tongue is "a restless evil, full of deadly poison" (3:8). Christians should follow wise leaders who display love and genuineness, not those whose speech is marked by slander and envy.

Words Reflect the Heart and Thus Manifest Consistency or Double-mindedness (3:9–12)

James concludes this section by warning of inconsistency and how it is displayed in words (3:9–12). He contends that this is unacceptable and shows that a stream of duplicitous words flows from a corrupt heart, whereas a pattern of wholesome speech emerges from a genuine heart.

8. James reflects Jesus' teaching that "what comes out of the mouth" is what "defiles a person" (Matt. 15:11).
9. Ralph P. Martin, *James*, Word Biblical Commentary (Waco, TX: Word, 1988), 115.
10. J. A. Motyer, *The Message of James*, Bible Speaks Today (Downers Grove, IL: InterVarsity Press, 1985), 123.

Revealing the unstable and deceitful nature of the tongue, James points out that double-minded people use the same tongue to (supposedly) worship God and to slander his people: "With it we bless our Lord and Father, and with it we curse people who are made in the likeness of God. From the same mouth come blessing and cursing. My brothers, these things ought not to be so" (3:9–10).

James illustrates this inconsistency with three questions that reveal the absurdity of the hypocritical use of the tongue (3:11–12). He asks if one spring supplies both fresh and bitter water, inquires whether a fig tree produces olives, and asks if a vine produces figs. Of course not; good springs produce good water, fig trees produce figs, and vines yield grapes and not figs. In other words, root determines fruit; the product comes from the source. Thus, following Jesus, James maintains that our words, which come from our heart, reveal much about our heart (cf. Matt. 7:16–20; 12:33–35; Luke 6:43–45). Negatively, poisonous words spew forth from a corrupt heart like a volcano erupting from beneath the earth's surface. Or, as Dale Ellenburg quips, "What's down in the well comes up in the bucket."

In the next paragraph (3:13–18), James links this principle with true and false wisdom and points out that not every leader who claims to have wisdom really does have it. This reiterates and expands his concern in 3:1. Not everyone should be a teacher, because not everyone has true wisdom. That more people claim to have true wisdom than actually possess it is obvious from the lack of control over their words and their overall lack of commitment to edify the church. Teachers exist to build up the church, not to harm it. And thus, those who are more interested in asserting themselves than in the unity of the body show that they value their own egos, ambitions, and agendas more than Christ's church. True wisdom, which is from God, is "first pure, then peaceable, gentle, open to reason, full of mercy and good fruits, impartial and sincere" (3:17). It does not exhibit bitter jealousy, selfish ambition, or pride, but shows itself in peaceable, kind, and meek words (3:13–18). Such wisdom comes from God, manifests itself

102

in a person's way of life and speech, and is prerequisite for teachers in Christ's churches.

Words of Slander Are Sinful and Will Be Judged (4:11–12; 5:9)

James 4 contrasts the peaceable fruit of wisdom with the presence of battles and factions in the churches being addressed. In a style reminiscent of the Old Testament prophets, James calls for repentance, demanding that these believers not quarrel with, slander, or judge one another (4:1–12). The references to quarrels, fights, war, and murder are not military but ecclesiastical. Martin notes: "Acrimonious speech, slanderous accusations, unrestrained anger—all depict a jealous and divided community; it speaks of a church governed by the 'wisdom from below.'"[11] James does not mince words as he forcefully addresses the sins of these covenant communities (4:1–2). There is discord and division in these churches, and James ties the problems to hypocrisy and pride. Some leaders of the church display hypocrisy by being preoccupied with the externals of religion without showing love for the poor or controlling their words. Their pride is seen by their willingness to disrupt the unity of the church in order to get their own way.

James links his pastoral and prophetic style and essentially says, "Repent because you are tearing apart the church by your internal strife and fighting." Solomon Andria captures James's perspective: "In the church, conflicts between people are not necessarily settled through negotiation, as would be the case in the political world. They are settled through repentance."[12]

James uses rhetorical questions to point to the seriousness of the churches' problems and their roots in selfishness, pride, and hypocrisy. He begins by showing these congregants that they "desire" something they lack (4:2). From the rest of the letter

11. Martin, *James*, 144.
12. Andria, "James," 1514.

and from 3:1 and 3:13–18, it seems best to conclude that they desire the power and influence of leadership (expressed in being a teacher, but probably also in other ways). They lack what they desire and may even feel left out or undervalued, so they "murder" (4:2). That is, they slander fellow church members who have the influence that they covet. They crave such influence, but cannot obtain it for themselves, so they "fight and quarrel" (4:2), creating conflicts in the church. But James ironically states that the reason they do not have such influence is that they do not ask for it (4:2). By this he means that they do not pray to the Lord in dependence, asking him for the very wisdom and maturity that would make them suitable leaders (cf. 1:5–8; 3:13–18). And when they do ask, they ask with the wrong motives, only wanting to indulge their evil desires (4:3). Interestingly, the double-minded do pray, but they pray in the same way that they live and speak: hypocritically and selfishly. Many of these double-minded church members are evidently praying to become leaders, not in order to serve the Lord, help the church, minister to the oppressed, and edify others, but in order to feel important and participate in significant decisions. They have turned everything upside down. Instead of seeking leadership for leadership's sake, people should want to exalt Jesus, edify the church, and serve others. Teachers, who will receive stricter judgment, should maintain this servant attitude, be wise, and display their wisdom by controlling their speech and by bringing peace.

One might suppose that since such errors are commonplace, James would go easy on these people. Instead, he calls them adulterers and therefore enemies of God (4:4). Jewish Christians certainly understood the metaphor of adultery, because it was used by the Old Testament prophets to speak of Israel as the covenant people who were unfaithful to the Lord and his covenant, even at times worshipping false gods (Hos. 9:1; Jer. 3; Isa. 54:5). The metaphor of adultery also makes sense in the New Testament, as the church is called the bride of Christ (Eph. 5:24–25). James confronts these congregants as spiritual adulterers because they are unfaithful to God and his covenant. They do not love God,

Christ's church, or the oppressed, but rather themselves, the world, and its systems of power.

James quotes Proverbs 3:34: "God opposes the proud, but gives grace to the humble" (4:6). In other words, the way to exaltation is not through self-promotion, but through humble service. Christians do not ascend into greatness, but descend, submitting to God and others. James no doubt reflects Jesus' emphasis and attitude here (cf. Matt. 20:20–28; Phil. 2:1–11). As Christians choose humility, they choose the path of grace and blessing. When people act in pride, they choose the route of divine wrath and resistance.

James then presents a series of imperatives that call for repentance. He initially commands his hearers to submit to God and resist the devil, the personal enemy of God and his people. They need to stop promoting themselves and instead align themselves with God and his revealed will. The command concerning the devil is explained by the connections between 4:6 and 4:7. In verse 6, James warns the churches that pride brings God's opposition, while humility brings God's blessings. In verse 7, James urges them to submit to God and thus embrace humility. In addition, they must resist the devil, who is the adversary, the accuser, or the slanderer. James, in effect, says: "When you slander other Christians, you are acting out of pride (which brings God's opposition) and following the example of the devil, the slanderer of God and his people. Repent. Stop following the devil's ways and start following God."

James then commands them to draw near to God and return to the Lord (4:8). If they do, they will find mercy. Zechariah held out God's similar invitation, "Return to me . . . and I will return to you" (Zech. 1:3). So did Isaiah: "Let the wicked forsake his way, and the unrighteous man his thoughts; let him return to the LORD, that he may have compassion on him, and to our God, for he will abundantly pardon" (Isa. 55:7). James subsequently pleads, "Cleanse your hands . . . and purify your hearts" (4:8). This resembles Psalm 24:3–4: "Who shall ascend the hill of the LORD? And who shall stand in his holy place? He who has clean hands and a pure heart, who does not lift up his soul to what is false and does not swear deceitfully." Ralph Martin suggests that "cleanse" and "purify" pertain to deeds and thoughts, respectively.[13] James is saying that his hearers must humble themselves, submit to God, resist the devil, draw near to God, cleanse their hands, purify their hearts, and even "be wretched and mourn and weep" (4:9). Their sin is serious and demands deep grief and sorrow. Such hypocrisy allows no room for levity.

James summarizes his commands, repeating in 4:10 his emphasis in 4:6, "Humble yourselves before the Lord, and he will exalt you" (cf. Matt. 23:12; Luke 14:11; 18:14; 1 Peter 5:6). The eschatological reversal is coming, James reminds us. Just as James 1:9–11 urges the lowly to boast in their exaltation and the rich in their humiliation, James 4:6 and 4:10 reminds us that the humble will be exalted and the proud opposed.

All this leads to James's point that we should not slander one another, because in so doing we are judging others—and ultimately ourselves. Martin rightly comments: "Any attitude that shows disdain or contempt for others reflects pride on the part of the one with the scornful attitude. This is characteristic of the double-minded person (4:8), who needs to exercise humility (4:6, 10)."[14] Conflicts in churches arise when members seek to get their own way at the expense of others. Church unity is tied to the people's humility before the Lord and others.

Based on the call for humility and the rebuke of pride, James commands tersely, "Do not speak evil against one another, brothers" (4:11). This recalls James 2:8–13 and the teachings of Leviticus 19: "You shall not go around as a slanderer among your people" (19:16). I-Jin Loh and Howard Hatton elucidate the command:

> The expression "speak evil against" is a single verb in Greek, literally "to talk (someone) down" or "to speak against." It is sometimes used of speaking against others behind their backs without giving them a chance to defend themselves, and there-

13. Martin, *James*, 153.
14. Ibid., 163.

fore has acquired the meaning of "speaking evil against" or "slander." In the New Testament it is sometimes listed as one of those vices and sins in the sense of false accusations (Rom. 1:30; 1 Pet. 2:1), and at other times it is used for harsh criticism or malicious accusation (2 Cor. 12:20; 1 Pet. 2:12; 3:16, "abused"). In the present context the verb is used in the sense of criticism or accusation made against others, and therefore it may be rendered as "criticize" (TEV), "slander" (NIV, NJB), "disparage" (NEB).[15]

James then explains the reason for his prohibition: those speaking evil against their fellow church members are actually speaking evil against the law itself, and even judging it (4:11). By disregarding the plain teachings of Leviticus 19 and of Jesus, these proud church members were presuming to have authority over the law. Those who judge the law are not doers of it (1:22–27), but sit in judgment against it, and, by implication, against God, who is the Lawgiver and Judge (4:12).[16] Andria states James's point in this way:

But [slander] is a dangerous game, for they [slanderers] are setting themselves up as judges and are judging others by their own set of standards. Judgment is God's prerogative, and he is the one who makes the laws. Usurping a function that is rightly his is sin (4:12). This sin encourages conflicts and open warfare within the community and clearly shows a failure to obey God's word, especially in relation to what it says about love for our neighbors.[17]

When people judge others and speak against them, they are in effect trying to push God off his judgment seat and place themselves on it. This is the height of presumption; God has unique

15. I-Jin Loh and Howard A. Hatton, *A Handbook on the Letter of James*, UBS Handbook Series (New York: United Bible Societies, 1997), 154–55.
16. The apostle Paul argues similarly. Romans 14:4 states: "Who are you to pass judgment on the servant of another? It is before his own master that he stands or falls." Romans 14:10 reiterates: "Why do you pass judgment on your brother? Or you, why do you despise your brother? For we will all stand before the judgment seat of God."
17. Andria, "James," 1514.

authority to give the law and to judge others according to it. Even more, God possesses the unique ability both to save and to destroy (4:12). Peter Davids points out the inherent inconsistency of slander: "The reason not to slander is that by attacking or setting oneself as a judge over a community member one is actually breaking the law which one claims to be upholding. If one can judge with respect to the law, one is no longer under the law but a judge."[18] James does not let people off the hook with the sin of slander. He considers it serious and rebukes it forcefully because he realizes that it is inevitably linked with judging others and flows from hypocrisy and pride. In this, he once more reflects Jesus:

> Judge not, that you be not judged. For with the judgment you pronounce you will be judged, and with the measure you use it will be measured to you. Why do you see the speck that is in your brother's eye, but do not notice the log that is in your own eye? Or how can you say to your brother, "Let me take the speck out of your eye," when there is the log in your own eye? You hypocrite, first take the log out of your own eye, and then you will see clearly to take the speck out of your brother's eye. (Matt. 7:1–5)

Words Must Display Submission to God, Not Pride or Boasting (4:13–17)

We unpacked this text when we examined James's teaching about the poor, so here we will consider only what it teaches concerning speech. The heart of the message of James 4:13–17 is that people's words sometimes express an unjustified confidence in the future that is in conflict with a genuine confidence in God. Words often display pride and presumption rather than what is truly appropriate—submission to and dependence upon God.

James makes this contrast plain by beginning 4:13 with "you who say" and 4:15 with "instead you ought to say." James instructs

18. Peter H. Davids, *The Epistle of James*, New International Greek Testament Commentary (Grand Rapids: Eerdmans, 1982), 169–70.

the churches to say, "If the Lord wills we will . . ." (4:15). The attitude reflected in this phrase displays a conscious awareness of God and his sovereignty, as well as our total dependence upon him. The point is not the phrase, for it too could become like the words condemned in James 2:14–17—pointless, religious clichés. Yet spoken from a genuine heart, such an expression of God's sovereignty and our submission could serve as a helpful reminder of God's truth for God's people (like praying, "in the name of Jesus"). Leaders in the New Testament church evidently used the expression (see Acts 18:21; 1 Cor. 4:19; 16:7; Phil. 2:19, 24; Heb. 6:3).

Unfortunately, the merchants did not express such dependence. James challenges them: "As it is, you boast in your arrogance. All such boasting is evil" (4:16). Boasting is routinely described as sin in the New Testament, except in cases where it is in Christ or his work. For example, James himself urges the poor to boast in their exaltation by God (1:9–11). In that case, boasting is appropriate because the idea is of rejoicing and glorying in God's eschatological reversal. But in James 4 the boasting is linked with the merchants' personal pride and presumption. Such boasting is sinful speech because it reflects a proud spirit, one of independence from God, not one of trust and submission.

Truthful Words Must Characterize God's People (5:12)

James 5:12 ("But above all, my brothers, do not swear . . .") has baffled interpreters for decades. The words "but above all" make it seem that James is culminating an argument, but it is hard to tell how this verse relates to James 5:7–11. At a minimum, it extends his emphasis on not grumbling and the coming judgment. Luke Johnson suggests that 5:12 marks a turn in the final section of the letter, and that James ends his letter emphasizing the positive ways in which words should be used in the community.[19] That seems to be the case in 5:13–20 and may fit 5:12 as well.

19. Luke Timothy Johnson, *The Letter of James*, The Anchor Bible (New York: Doubleday, 1995), 325–26.

By beginning with "above all," James links this verse to previous material and highlights the significance of the subsequent truth:[20] tell the truth in a straightforward manner, avoiding oaths, because judgment is coming. James 5:12 stresses this with a prohibition, an instruction, and a rationale. James cautions, "Do not swear, either by heaven or by earth or by any other oath" (5:12). This does not refer to "cursing" or swearing in the four-letter-word sense (although that would violate Ephesians 4:29–5:4), but in the sense of promising by something to guarantee one's word.

Interestingly, Leviticus 19, the passage to which James refers again and again, also commands telling the truth and not swearing falsely by oaths: "You shall not steal; you shall not deal falsely; you shall not lie to one another. You shall not swear by my name falsely, and so profane the name of your God: I am the LORD" (19:11–12). Especially important to understanding James 5:12, though, are Jesus' words in the Sermon on the Mount, a portion of which James quotes virtually verbatim:

> Again you have heard that it was said to those of old, "You shall not swear falsely, but shall perform to the Lord what you have sworn." But I say to you, Do not take an oath at all, either by heaven, for it is the throne of God, or by the earth, for it is his footstool, or by Jerusalem, for it is the city of the great King. And do not take an oath by your head, for you cannot make one hair white or black. Let what you say be simply "Yes" or "No"; anything more than this comes from evil. (Matt. 5:33–37)

Important for understanding Jesus' words in Matthew 5 are his criticisms of the hypocrisy of the scribes and Pharisees:

> Woe to you, blind guides, who say, "If anyone swears by the temple, it is nothing, but if anyone swears by the gold of the temple, he is bound by his oath." You blind fools! For which is greater, the gold or the temple that has made the gold sacred? And you say, "If anyone swears by the altar, it is nothing, but

---

20. See William R. Baker, "'Above All Else': Contexts of the Call for Verbal Integrity in James 5:12," *Journal for the Study of the New Testament* 54 (1994): 57–71.

if anyone swears by the gift that is on the altar, he is bound by his oath." You blind men! For which is greater, the gift or the altar that makes the gift sacred? So whoever swears by the altar swears by it and by everything on it. And whoever swears by the temple swears by it and by him who dwells in it. And whoever swears by heaven swears by the throne of God and by him who sits upon it. (Matt. 23:16–22)

Evidently, Jesus' rebukes of oaths are particularly designed to challenge the elaborate first-century Jewish customs of oath-taking and their attempt to get around the misuse of God's name by referring instead to things that would symbolize God or his rule—like heaven, the earth, Jerusalem, or even one's own head.

James's intention is similar. Ben Witherington observes:

The point of oaths is to swear the truth to some remark, which implies the general unreliableness of all remarks without oaths. James, like his brother, indicates that Christians should be without need of such devices and should mean what they say and say what they mean all the time without duplicity or outright falsehood. This is part of being a sincere and honest Christian. Someone who abuses or even uses such oaths is in danger of accountability at the judgment. Better to not invoke God in this way than call down judgment on oneself.[21]

James not only prohibits the swearing of oaths, but instructs his hearers to "let your 'yes' be yes and your 'no' be no" (5:12). Like Jesus in Matthew 5:37, James calls for straightforward and honest speech. Consistent people have no need to swear oaths, because their word is good without them.

James advises this simple truth-telling "so that you may not fall under condemnation" (5:12). As we noted earlier, God will judge our speech and our actions (James 2:8–13). Indeed, every word that is spoken will be judged, Jesus cautions (Matt. 12:36–37). To say yes and mean no, or to say no and mean yes, is to lie. But

21. Ben Witherington III, *Letters and Homilies for Jewish Christians: A Socio-Rhetorical Commentary on Hebrews, James and Jude* (Downers Grove, IL: InterVarsity Press, 2007), 539.

to manipulate language in such a way as to make our words seem to mean one thing, when we really mean something else, is also to lie. It is also hypocrisy, which by nature leads to flattery and double-talk, rather than honest speech. Such dishonest speech is a reflection of a hypocritical, double-minded heart; honest speech reflects a genuine heart with nothing to hide or twist.

Words Must Edify the Church (5:13-20)

Thus far, James's discussion of words has been largely negative. But in James 5:13–20 the emphasis is positive. James concludes his epistle by emphasizing how the community of faith is supposed to operate. Churches can be strengthened as the people of God use their words to pray, praise, confess, and restore. In so doing, they help the sick, encourage others, point to forgiveness, and even restore wanderers.

When someone in the church is suffering, he should pray (5:13). James does not specify what suffering he has in mind. It may be the persecution and oppression he discusses in 1:2–11 and 5:1–6. Or he may be pointing to general afflictions. Either way, James instructs his hearers to pray. They are not to grumble or seek revenge, but turn to God.

When someone in the church is cheerful, he should sing praises (5:13). When things seem to be going wrong, our words can be used for good—we can pray. When the blessings of God seem to be poured out all around us, our words can be used for good—we can sing joyfully.

And when someone in the church is sick, he should call for the elders to come and pray over him. Times of sickness often make people feel helpless and hopeless, as if there is nothing they can do. But James reminds us that there is something that sick people can do. They can pray, and they can ask their church leaders to pray for them (5:14). Thankfully, God answers prayer, forgives confessed sin, and heals the sick. Thus, our words can be used for our good and for the good of others in the church.

Words are also to be used for confessing our sins to one another and praying for one another (5:16). James longs for churches to be characterized by transparency, not hypocrisy. That would facilitate the confession of sins, which would keep the community healthy. Consistent followers of Jesus are humble, honest, and merciful, and they genuinely desire to help others. As a result, they do not look for faults in others, seek to use their mistakes against them, or slander them. In contrast, hypocrites, who are proud, judgmental, and prone to slander, want others to think more highly of them than is realistic. Confessing our sins to hypocrites will result in that honesty being used against us, whereas confessing our sins to genuine, consistent followers of Christ will result in sharing life with people who will help us become more mature.

James concludes his letter with a plea to rescue those who are straying from the truth. Commentators disagree on the identity of these wanderers—are they fellow believers who have fallen by the wayside, or are they unbelievers still in their sin? Most likely, they are a part of visible churches, though the genuineness of their salvation is yet to be proven. James longs for the people in these churches to seek the restoration of these wanderers (cf. Gal. 6:1–10). From what we have seen in James's instructions so far, it is quite likely that many in these churches were failing to help these spiritual drifters. Many were too busy slandering each other, trying to promote themselves and their friends into leadership positions, and arguing about the particulars of how to perform their religion well. People headed for destruction were largely forgotten—after all, there were ministry positions to seek! But the pastoral heart of James keeps pressing the people of God to use their words appropriately—not to tear down the church, but to help others, edify the body, and restore those who wander.

9

God's Word and Law

WHILE JAMES'S READERS were people of words, he longed for them to be people of God's word. James speaks of God's word as "the word of truth" (1:18), "the implanted word" (1:21), and "the word" (1:22, 23). He speaks of God's law as "the perfect law" (1:25), "the law of liberty" (1:25; 2:12), "the royal law" (2:8), and simply "the law" (2:9, 10, 11; 4:11). He also refers to "the Scripture" (2:8, 23; 4:5), Old Testament material (such as Abraham, Rahab, Elijah, the prophets, Job, Exodus 20, Leviticus 19, and Deuteronomy), and Jesus' teachings. How these terms and ideas relate to one another is exceedingly complex. For example, what does James mean by God's "word"? Is it the same as his "law"? How does the perfect law of liberty fit into this? Does James have Leviticus 19 in mind, or the teachings of Jesus, or something broader? A variety of answers to such important questions are given. Unfortunately, too often they are so entangled with questions related to the identity of word and law that there is a failure to state what we can and do know about James's theology of the word and law. While we will address the above questions, we will focus on key texts and teachings related to word and law in James:

- The Word Is Truthful (1:18).
- "The Word of Truth" Is Used by God to Bring Us Forth as the New Creation (1:18).

115

- The Expressions "Word" and "Law" Are Used Broadly and Somewhat Interchangeably (1:19–25).
- The Word Is Authoritative for Belief and Behavior (1:19–25).
- The Law Is "Perfect" (1:25).
- The Law Is "The Law of Liberty" (1:25; cf. 2:12).
- "The Implanted Word" Must Be Received (1:21).
- God Blesses Those Who Hear and Practice the Word (1:22–25).
- The Word Has a Holistic Role in the Lives of God's People (1:18–25).
- The Law Is "Royal" and Tied to Jesus and the Kingdom (2:8).
- The Law Will Serve as a Basis for the Last Judgment (2:8–13; 4:11–12).
- The Law Is a Unity (2:8–13).
- The Law Communicates the Will of God as the Lawgiver (2:8–13; 4:11–12).

The Word Is Truthful (1:18)

James writes of "the word of truth," drawing attention to the veracity of the word (the word which is true) or the truthful content of the word (the word contains truth). This phrase has been variously identified by interpreters as the Old Testament, Christ himself, or the gospel. In the Old Testament, God's word is often described as true (Deut. 22:20; 2 Sam. 7:28; Pss. 15:2; 118:43; Jer. 23:28; Prov. 22:21). Jesus also taught that he is the truth (John 14:6) and that God's word is truth (John 17:17). Yet "the word of truth" can refer to the gospel, as in Ephesians 1:13 (cf. Col. 1:5) and 2 Timothy, where Paul uses "word" to refer to both the gospel and the Old Testament (2:9, 15; 4:2). Peter apparently speaks of the word similarly—as the gospel and as the Old Testament

(1 Peter 1:23–25).[1] Peter O'Brien states that this usage of "word" is part and parcel of the early Christian mission terminology.[2] So although we do not know precisely how James intends for us to understand this term, he seems to use "the word of truth" here in a way that links the Old Testament and the gospel, and likely the teachings of Jesus.

"The Word of Truth" Is Used by God to Bring Us Forth as the New Creation (1:18)

God uses the word of truth to bring us forth into a new creation (1:18). James and Peter again appear similar, as Peter teaches that "you have been born again, not of perishable seed but of imperishable, through the living and abiding word of God" (1 Peter 1:23). Paul likewise points to the word and the gospel as God-ordained means to bring people to saving faith (Rom. 1:16–17; 10:13–17; Eph. 1:13). While both Peter (1 Peter 1:3–5) and Paul link the new birth to our union with the resurrected Christ (Eph. 2:1–10), James's particular concern in 1:18 is to contrast the word of truth as an instrument of life with sin as an instrument that results in death (1:13–18). In contrast to the desire that brings forth sin, the word of truth brings forth a new creation. The word functions as God's seed that brings about God's purposes. The context also implies that the word of truth is one of the good and perfect gifts that come down from above.[3]

Such an emphasis on the word's goodness, divine origin, and life-giving power echoes the Old Testament. Furthermore, the understanding of God's word as a means of his creation (Gen. 1; Pss. 33:6–9; 104:7) is similar to James's teaching of the word's creative role in bringing forth the new creation. Horton ably expresses

1. Karen H. Jobes, *1 Peter*, Baker Exegetical Commentary on the New Testament (Grand Rapids: Baker, 2005), 123–41.
2. Peter T. O'Brien, *The Letter to the Ephesians*, Pillar New Testament Commentary (Grand Rapids: Eerdmans, 1999), 118–20.
3. Luke Timothy Johnson, "Mirror of Remembrance (James 1:22–25)," *Catholic Biblical Quarterly* 50 (1988): 632–45.

the active nature of God's word: "God's *speaking* is *acting*, and this acting is not only descriptive and propositional; it is also creative and performative."[4] The gospel is more than God's invitation to sinners to come into communion with Christ; it is itself the effective means by which God brings about this goal (cf. Heb. 4:12–13; Rom. 1:16; 10:17).[5] In other words, James teaches that we are on the receiving end as the new creation. To be sure, we are not passive in our faith, but we are not the causative agents, either. Like the word and through the word, our salvation always comes first from outside us and then to and into us.

The Expressions "Word" and "Law" Are Used Broadly and Somewhat Interchangeably (1:19–25)

There is no consensus on what James means by "the law." M. J. Evans lists several views: (1) no identifiable content, (2) the Old Testament Torah, (3) the Old Testament as a whole, (4) the Ten Commandments and other ethical precepts, (5) Leviticus 19, (6) teachings of Jesus, (7) the fulfilled law as personified by Jesus, and (8) a combination of the Old Testament and the teachings of Jesus.[6]

While a detailed interaction with these views goes beyond our purposes, I will offer a brief rationale for my position. First, however we understand James's concept of the word, we must link it to his understanding of the law, which is likened to a mirror in James 1:23 and called "the perfect law" as well as "the law of liberty" in 1:25. James begins this section by emphasizing the importance of doing the word and ends with a blessing on those who do the law. He thereby treats them as fundamentally synonymous.[7]

4. Michael S. Horton, *People and Place: A Covenant Ecclesiology* (Louisville, KY: Westminster John Knox, 2008), 39 (emphasis in original).

5. Ibid., 41.

6. M. J. Evans, "The Law in James," *Vox Evangelica* 13 (1983): 29–40.

7. This argument is developed by Mariam Kamell, "The Word/Law in James as the Promised New Covenant," paper presented in the Scripture and Early Judaism session of the Society of Biblical Literature Annual Meeting, November 19, 2006.

Further, James's use of the term "law" reflects his Jewish understanding of the law as Torah. But his understanding of the Torah was also linked to his belief in the authority of the entire Hebrew Bible, so the broadening of the law to include the Old Testament in general seems appropriate. We noted earlier that James roots many of his ideas in the Old Testament law, prophets, and wisdom literature and regards the whole Old Testament as authoritative. Yet, as we will see, James focuses his discussion of the law in 2:8–13 on the Ten Commandments and Leviticus 19. So a view that highlights his emphasis on these two pivotal texts is insightful. Yet even they are discussed alongside "a number of Gospel categories."[8]

In addition, James's continual references to the teachings of Jesus, the royal law, the perfect law, the law of liberty, and the centrality of love in his discussions make it likely that he has Jesus' teachings in mind as well. Plus, his use of the phrase "the word of truth" reflects a wide apostolic usage and likely highlights the gospel itself.

Because of all of this, I suggest that James's references to "the law" are not as narrowly focused as some have asserted. Instead, he uses the terms "word" and "law" somewhat interchangeably, and both terms appear to depict broadly the Old Testament, key ethical teachings in the Old Testament, and the new covenant promise revealed in the gospel and the teachings of Jesus (1:19–25).[9]

The Word Is Authoritative for Belief and Behavior (1:19–25)

James does not view the word or the law as a relic of the old covenant, but as crucial, relevant, and authoritative for Christians and churches. It must be heard and obeyed, as we see spelled out in several of the remaining principles.

8. D. A. Carson, "James," in *Commentary on the New Testament Use of the Old Testament*, ed. D. A. Carson and G. K. Beale (Grand Rapids: Baker, 2007), 1000.
9. Cf. James 5:19–20, where "the truth" evidently references the overall gospel and Christian faith and life.

The Law Is "Perfect" (1:25)

How is the law "perfect"? Recall that James has already used the word "perfect" in 1:4 and 1:17. James 1:4 uses it in reference to the eschatological completeness produced by perseverance amidst trials. James 1:17 speaks of God as the giver of every good and perfect gift, and in context that seems to refer to salvation and our role as the firstfruits of creation. Robert Wall proposes that the phrase "the perfect law" expresses the eschatological flavor of James's wider teaching on perfection. That is, the perfect law "purposes an eschatological and redemptive effect for those who obey its command."[10] While that interpretation correctly points to an important function of the law in James, it is more natural to see James's primary emphasis on the Old Testament teaching in Psalms 19 and 119 (cf. Rom. 7:12). For example, Psalm 19:7–11 states:

> The law of the LORD is perfect,
>   reviving the soul;
> the testimony of the LORD is sure,
>   making wise the simple;
> the precepts of the LORD are right,
>   rejoicing the heart;
> the commandment of the LORD is pure,
>   enlightening the eyes;
> the fear of the LORD is clean,
>   enduring forever;
> the rules of the LORD are true,
>   and righteous altogether.
> More to be desired are they than gold,
>   even much fine gold;
> sweeter also than honey
>   and drippings of the honeycomb.
> Moreover, by them is your servant warned;
>   in keeping them there is great reward.

10. Robert W. Wall, *Community of the Wise: The Letter of James*, New Testament in Context (Valley Forge, PA: Trinity Press International, 1997), 97.

In continuity with Psalm 19, James highlights not only the idea of the law's perfection, but also interrelated themes of life, wisdom, joy, purity, cleanness, righteousness, and reward.[11]

Peter Davids adds that the perfect law may point to the eschatological nature of Jesus' role and teaching, for he gives a new and perfected law (cf. Matt. 5–7, especially 5:17).[12] This especially makes sense of James's other depictions of the law, as we will see.

The Law Is "the Law of Liberty" (1:25; cf. 2:12)

To modern ears, "the law of liberty" sounds like an oxymoron. Laws are thought to limit rather than advance freedom. James stands in the tradition of the Old Testament writers who depict God's word as fostering our well-being, healing us, refreshing us, giving us life, and sustaining us (cf. Deut. 8:3; 32:1–2; Pss. 119; 107:20; Ezek. 37:4–14). Ralph Martin explains, "This implies that we are set free from ourselves to serve our neighbors. . . . [I]t connotes a release from self-interest and a new capacity to practice God's will in the interests of one's needy neighbors."[13] While it is plausible that James derived the notion of the law of liberty solely from his Jewish roots, it seems more likely that he takes the Jewish ideals related to God's law and interprets them eschatologically, in light of the new covenant fulfilled in Christ.[14]

"The Implanted Word" Must Be Received (1:21)

Douglas Moo's comments on James 1:21 are insightful:

The word is not something that all people have within them from birth onward, but an entity that has taken up residence

---

11. I owe this insight to Mariam Kamell through personal correspondence.

12. Peter H. Davids, *The Epistle of James*, New International Greek Testament Commentary (Grand Rapids: Eerdmans, 1982), 99.

13. Ralph P. Martin, *James*, Word Biblical Commentary (Waco: Word, 1988), 51.

14. The linking of the love command to the law in James 2:8–13 resembles Jesus' teaching. Cf. Gal. 5:1–14; Rom. 8:1–4; 13:8–10.

within believers. James likely draws this striking conception of the implanted word from the famous new covenant prophecy of Jeremiah 31. The prophet, noting the failure of Israel to live up to the terms of the Mosaic covenant, announces on behalf of God a new covenant that God would enter into with his people. As a prominent component of that new covenant arrangement, God promises to put his law within his people, to write it on their hearts (Jer. 31:33). . . . James's language reminds his readers that they have experienced the fulfillment of that wonderful promise. But it also reminds them that the word that has saved them cannot be dispensed with after conversion. God plants it within his people, making it a permanent, inseparable part of the believer, a guiding and commanding presence within.[15]

"The implanted word" could also allude to Deuteronomy 30, where Moses instructs the people that God has placed the word into their mouths and hearts (30:14).

Interestingly, James continues his imagery of the word as seed. While he later likens the word to a mirror that corrects those who look into it (1:23), here he compares it again to a seed in the soil of the believer's heart (cf. Jesus' teaching in Matt. 13:1–23). Previously, the seed was God's instrument to bring us forth into a new creation (1:16–18), and here it is God's agent by which he shapes believers. This word, like every good and perfect gift, comes down from God and is received by us. Thus, the word is not innate within us. It is external to us before God implants it within us.

God Blesses Those Who Hear and Practice the Word (1:22–25)

As we saw above, James again sounds the note of Jesus, "Blessed rather are those who hear the word of God and keep it" (Luke 11:28). Indeed, the Sermon on the Mount begins and ends with an emphasis on the eschatological blessing of God, and Jesus

15. Douglas J. Moo, *The Letter of James*, Pillar New Testament Commentary (Grand Rapids: Eerdmans, 2000), 87.

concludes his message by urging obedience to his teachings. Those who hear and practice them enter the kingdom and experience eschatological and covenantal blessings, but those who hear his words without doing them will receive covenant curses, suffering banishment and destruction (Matt. 7:21–27; cf. Deut. 30:1–20).

The Word Has a Holistic Role in the Lives of God's People (1:18–25)

Just as God's word is his agency throughout the biblical story of creation, election, redemption, and the new creation, so also he uses the word holistically in the lives of his people. Through his word, God brings believers forth into a new creation (1:18) and brings about their final salvation (1:21). Because of this, believers are to "be quick to hear" the word (1:19), to lay aside sin in preparation for receiving the word (1:21), to receive it with meekness (1:21), and to hear and do it (1:22–25). Believers who do the word will be blessed in their doing (1:25). Thus, God uses the word at the beginning, the middle, and the end of the Christian life. At each step on the journey, the people of God must submit their thinking and lives to God's authoritative word.

The Law Is "Royal" and Tied to Jesus and the Kingdom (2:8)

"Royal" means belonging to the king or the kingdom. This idea flows from James 2:1–7, where James stresses loving the poor, who are chosen by God and heirs of the kingdom. It is also attached to the command to love one's neighbor as oneself in Leviticus 19:18, which Jesus taught was the center of the entire law:

> But when the Pharisees heard that he had silenced the Saddu-
> cees, they gathered together. And one of them, a lawyer, asked
> him a question to test him. "Teacher, which is the great com-
> mandment in the Law?" And he said to him, "You shall love the

Lord your God with all your heart and with all your soul and with all your mind. This is the great and first commandment. And a second is like it: You shall love your neighbor as yourself. On these two commandments depend all the Law and the Prophets." (Matt. 22:34–40; cf. 5:17–20; Luke 10:25–37)

Moo explains the idea this way:

> James intends "royal" to connote the law pertaining to the kingdom of God. As with the phrase "the perfect law that gives freedom" in 1:25, then "royal law" might be James's way of referring to the sum total of demands that God, through Jesus, imposes on believers: "the whole law as interpreted and handed over to the church in the teaching of Jesus." Understood in this sense, the "royal law" may well extend beyond the Mosaic law as fulfilled and reinterpreted by Jesus to include the teaching of Jesus.[16]

The Law Will Serve as a Basis for the Last Judgment (2:8-13; 4:11-12)

James assumes that the law still has authority—the prohibitions of murder and adultery stand. He also straightforwardly points to the law's ability to be a standard that convicts those who transgress it. Then upon that foundation, James asserts that we should speak and act as those who will be judged by the law of liberty. The law communicates God's will and standards, and, as such, it will be a basis for the eschatological judgment (cf. Rom. 2:12).

The Law Is a Unity (2:8-13)

It is easy for us in contemporary society to think of the law as a series of individual commands that relate to a variety of spheres. Because of this, we tend to think that breaking one com-

16. Moo, *James*, PNTC, 112. Moo quotes Davids, *James*, 114.

mand has very little to do with the others. Not so, according to James. Rather, the particular laws are understood holistically, as linked to covenant faithfulness, and as expressing the will of one Lawgiver. To violate any command is to display unfaithfulness to God and his covenant. "A rock thrown through a window strikes the glass at only one point, but it can cause the whole window to shatter. So it is with the law."[17] The reason for this lies in the next principle.

The Law Communicates the Will of God as the Lawgiver (2:8-13; 4:11-12)

"He who said" (2:11) emphasizes that this is *God's* law. It has authority because of the One who uttered it. Critical to the argument is that we have God speaking through the law. This idea is foundational for some of James's other principles concerning the law. The law is truthful because God is truthful. It is perfect because God effectively accomplishes his purposes through it. It is authoritative because it expresses God's will. It is an instrument in our salvation because God saves us in part through revealing himself to us. It serves as a basis of our judgment because the Lawgiver is the Judge (cf. 4:11–12). The law is a unity because it comes from one Lawgiver: God.

James's view of word and law is a part of his larger theology of revelation and Scripture. The ways in which he refers to the Law, the Prophets, and the Wisdom Literature (the Writings) display his conviction that they possess abiding authority for the churches in theology and practice. Unmistakably, the Old Testament in all its parts still carries authority for the church.

James's belief that the Old Testament remains authoritative for the church is even more striking when it is coupled with his frequent use of Jesus' teachings as authoritative. Along with the Old Testament, the teachings of Jesus form the basis of many of

17. Christopher W. Morgan and B. Dale Ellenburg, *James: Wisdom for the Community* (Fearn, UK: Christian Focus Publications, 2008), 100.

James's exhortations to the churches. It is significant in the development of the canon and the doctrine of Scripture that James considers the teachings of Jesus as authoritative for these churches. As an influential leader of the Jerusalem church, James reflects, and may have been a key leader in shaping, the early Christian belief that Jesus' teachings bear divine authority. This is no small point: one of the earliest Christian leaders in one of the earliest Christian documents holds that both the entire Old Testament and the teachings of Jesus bear abiding authority and relevance for the church's beliefs and behavior.

10

James and Paul

JAMES AND PAUL make these statements about justification:

> You see that a person is justified by works and not by faith alone. (James 2:24)

> For we hold that one is justified by faith apart from works of the law. (Romans 3:28)

Do these verses constitute a contradiction in Scripture? Does James refute Paul's teaching on justification, or vice versa? What are we to think about this theological dilemma?

This issue actually turns on three related but distinct questions. First is the historical question: to what teaching is James responding? In other words, is James addressing the claims of Paul, a misunderstanding of Paul, or something else altogether? Second is the theological question: what is James actually teaching concerning justification, faith, and works?[1] Third is the canonical question: are the teachings of James and Paul compatible or inconsistent? Too often people begin by asking the canonical question. However, Adolf Schlatter appropriately warns, "It does not make any sense to compare James to Paul before at least James has been understood."[2] Careful theological method requires that we examine the historical

---

1. This framework expands on that of Richard Bauckham, *James: Wisdom of James, Disciple of Jesus the Sage* (London: Routledge, 1999), 119.
2. I owe this quote to Bauckham, *James*, 119.

question first, then the theological question, and only upon that foundation are we capable of answering the canonical question.

- The Historical Question: To What Teaching Is James Responding?
- The Theological Question: What Does James 2:14–26 Teach?
- The Canonical Question: Are the Teachings of James and Paul Compatible?

The Historical Question: To What Teaching Is James Responding?

Major Views

James vs. Paul. Three types of answers have been given to the historical question. One view is that James is responding to Paul's teaching on justification. We might call it the "James vs. Paul" view. The great Reformer Martin Luther is the most well-known defender of this view. Focused so intently on refuting the Roman Catholic Church's teaching on salvation as connected to the church, the sacraments, and good works, Luther embraced Paul's teaching on justification but rejected that of James. Luther concluded that while John, Romans, Galatians, Ephesians, and 1 Peter "show you Christ and teach you all that is necessary and salvatory for you to know . . . St. James's epistle really is an epistle of straw, compared to these others, for it has nothing of the nature of the gospel about it."[3] Luther maintained that James "is flatly against St. Paul and all the rest of Scripture in ascribing justification to works [2:24]. It says that Abraham was justified by his works . . . [2:21]; though in Romans 4[:2–22] St. Paul teaches to the contrary

3. *Martin Luther's Basic Theological Writings*, ed. Timothy F. Lull (Minneapolis: Fortress, 1989), 117; see also Timothy George, "'A Right Strawy Epistle': Reformation Perspectives on James," *The Southern Baptist Journal of Theology* 4, no. 3 (Fall 2000): 20–31.

that Abraham was justified apart from works, by his faith alone, before he had offered his son."[4] The critical scholar F. C. Baur also represents this view. Baur believed that James, a proponent of Jewish Christianity, stood opposed to Paul, the apostle to the Gentiles. According to this view, James's and Paul's teachings are contradictory and intentionally so. Thus, any attempt to harmonize them is misguided.[5]

James vs. Paulinism. A second common response to the historical question is that James addresses people who have misunderstood Paul's view of justification by faith and have fallen into some sort of antinomianism, possibly overemphasizing freedom in Christ to the point that obedience to Christ was not mandatory. This might be called the "James vs. Paulinism" view. According to this view, there is no need to see a conflict between James and Paul because James does not have Paul's theology in mind. James is critiquing some who have taken Paul's idea and distorted it to the point that good works are unnecessary in following Christ. Most holding to the James vs. Paulinism view would seem to suggest a late date for the epistle of James (enough time for followers of Paul to distort his teaching) and therefore a different author than James, the brother of Jesus.[6] John Piper, however, holds this position but maintains the traditional view of authorship and date. He says, "James is not contradicting Paul here but teaching something compatible with Paul's teaching and correcting a misuse of Paul's teaching. Paul was very aware that his

4. *Luther's Works: Word and Sacrament* (Philadelphia: Muhlenberg, 1960), 35:396.

5. Scholars who follow this "conflict" view include G. Lüdemann, M. Goulder, and M. Hengel. See G. Lüdemann, *Opposition to Paul in Jewish Christianity*, trans. M. E. Boring (Minneapolis: Fortress, 1989); M. Goulder, *A Tale of Two Missions* (London: SCM Press, 1994); M. Hengel, *The "Hellenization" of Judaea in the First Century after Christ*, trans. J. Bowden (Philadelphia: Trinity Press International, 1989).

6. See chapter 1 on "James in Context" for more on the issues related to date and authorship. Scholars who hold a version of this view include Leonard Goppelt, *Theology of the New Testament* (Grand Rapids: Eerdmans, 1982), 2:209; W. Marxsen, *Introduction to the New Testament* (Philadelphia: Fortress, 1970), 230–31; C. Leslie Mitton, *The Epistle of James* (Grand Rapids: Eerdmans, 1966), 8. See other references in Robert H. Stein, "'Saved by Faith [Alone]' in Paul versus 'Not Saved by Faith Alone' in James," *The Southern Baptist Journal of Theology* 4, no. 3 (Fall 2000): 4–19.

teaching of justification by faith alone was being distorted and misused."[7] Piper references Romans 3:8; 5:20; 6:1 and Galatians 5:13 as examples of Paul's responses to such distortions. Paul had to regularly maintain that his understanding of grace leads to obedience and does not provide a license to sin.

James without Reference to Paul. The third major answer given to the historical question is what we call the "James without reference to Paul" view. According to it, James addresses the issue of justification in a different context than Paul. James focuses on the nature of genuine faith. People with genuine faith overcome trials, are doers of the word, take care of the oppressed, control their speech, exemplify holy living, are deeply interested in the poor, etc. James 2:14–26 follows this train of thought and shows that true faith does not merely offer verbal platitudes to the poor, but actively expresses itself in works of love. This genuine faith is vindicated by corresponding works. Paul, on the other hand, when speaking about justification, faith, and works, is usually focusing on the salvation of the Gentiles. Paul seeks to protect the doctrine of grace, emphasizing that Gentiles may become Christians through faith in Christ and not by performing good deeds or adopting Jewish identity markers like circumcision, Sabbath keeping, and food laws. Proponents of this view argue that apart from the verbal similarity between Paul and James, there is actually very little contextual resemblance.[8]

Analysis

Personal Conclusions. I find the James vs. Paul view too quick to suppose conflict. The historical acceptance of James as

---

7. John Piper, "Does James Contradict Paul?" sermon delivered August 8, 1999. Available online at www.desiringgod.org (and at the time of this publication, at www.desiring god.org/ResourceLibrary/Sermons/ByDate/1999/1085_Does_James_Contradict_Paul).

8. Stein, "'Saved by Faith [Alone],'" 4–19; Ronald Y. K. Fung, "'Justification' in the Epistle of James," in *Right with God: Justification in the Bible and the World*, ed. D. A. Carson (Grand Rapids: Baker, 1992), 146–62.

canonical, the theological importance of the unity of Scripture, and a rejection of the notion of a canon within the canon all militate against the James vs. Paul view.[9] Luke relates that Paul and James were in agreement on the issues of justification by faith, the inclusion of Gentiles in the church, and the observance of Jewish regulations (Acts 15). In addition, if James was seeking to set Paul and his theology straight in terms of the law and its requirements, then James failed to do so. James simply does not address key issues that would be at the heart of such a dispute with Paul, such as the place of circumcision, Sabbath keeping, food laws, and other ceremonial laws. A careful reading of James and Paul shows that they are dealing with different matters and different false teachings.

The James vs. Paulinism view is potentially fruitful, since Acts 21:17–26 indicates that James warned Paul that many misunderstood his view of the law. It would not be hard to see how some would have extended that misunderstanding to Paul's teaching on justification. As Piper observes, Paul himself seems to recognize this possibility. Most teachers know the frustration of having students misinterpret or distort their teachings. This view makes sense of the issues. Yet, as mentioned previously, if James was addressing even a distortion of Paul's doctrine of justification, then he would have been expected to address key issues like circumcision, Sabbath keeping, and food laws, which seem to be at the center of the tensions in Acts 15 and 21. This omission is conceivable only if the distortions of Paul's view did not pertain to such concerns.

But is it necessary to suppose that James is responding to Paul or a distortion of his teachings? The two primary reasons why some suppose that there is this connection are the tradition set by Luther and the striking similarity in terminology. Concerning the tradition, Richard Bauckham laments that both the James vs. Paul view and the James vs. Paulinism view require James to be interpreted "in a historical position relative to Paul

---

9. Each of the biblical writings should be interpreted first on its own terms, not primarily in the light of Pauline terminology.

and Paulinism."[10] He follows Johnson, who likewise complains that scholars continue to read what is different from Paul with primary reference to him, rather than understanding James and other such material simply as having different emphases.[11]

Rather than having Paul or a distortion of Pauline theology in view, James is more likely, when discussing justification, simply developing his own points regarding the Old Testament and especially the teachings of Jesus. That would be consistent with the indications of an early date of James's writing; it would also be more consistent with the other themes found in James (as discussed in the previous chapters). While an emphasis on faith and the necessity of corresponding obedience is found in the Old Testament, a quick glance at the teachings of Jesus shows that James is likely following his trajectory. The obedient will be blessed in their doing (James 1:25; John 13:17). True religion is more than external observances; it is also a matter of full obedience, which includes the heart (James 1:26–27; Matt. 6:1–18). Love of God and others is central to Christianity—believing the facts is not enough (James 2:8; Matt. 22:34–40). Note especially how James 2:14–26 resembles the teaching of Jesus that final salvation is evidenced in showing works of love for fellow believers (Matt. 25:34–46). Jesus condemns religious hypocrisy (Matt. 6:1–18) and warns that a mere profession of faith will not result in justification at the last judgment (Matt. 7:21–23). He also states that fruit will evidence one's faith (Matt. 7:16–20), that his true followers hear and obey (Matt. 7:24–27), and that judgment will be according to works (Matt. 16:27).

Potential Objections. What about the remarkable similarity in terminology between James and Paul? And what about the reference to Abraham in both of their arguments? Robert Stein helpfully examines the differences in terminology.[12] He looks at how James and Paul use "faith/believe" as well as "works." He notes that James

10. Bauckham, *James*, 119.
11. Ibid; Luke Timothy Johnson, *The Letter of James*, The Anchor Bible (New York: Doubleday, 1995), 191.
12. Stein, "'Saved by Faith [Alone],'" 5–8.

employs the noun "faith" sixteen times—five times outside this passage (1:3, 6; 2:1, 5; 5:15) and the rest in 2:14–26. The verb "believe" is used only three times in James—all three times in 2:14–26. With the exception of its usage in 2:14–26, faith in James always has positive connotations: faith during trials (1:3), praying in faith (1:6; 5:15), faith in/of Christ (2:1), and the poor as rich in faith (2:5). Faith in these passages is assumed to be genuine. Faith is more than intellectual assent to doctrinal truths, and includes an element of personal trust and commitment to God. When James discusses "faith" in 2:14–26, however, he is engaging a real or imaginary opponent (this argument is called a "diatribe") over the nature of faith. That James differs with this opponent over the nature of faith is clear for each reference to faith in the passage, as Stein notes:

> 2:14a—It is a faith that possesses no works.
> 2:14b—It is a faith that cannot save.
> 2:17—It is a faith without works that is dead.
> 2:18a—It is a faith that is distinct and separate from works.
> 2:18b—It is a faith that is contrasted with works.
> 2:18c—It is contrasted with a faith shown by works.
> 2:20—It is a faith without works that is useless.
> 2:22a—It is contrasted with a faith that is active along with works.
> 2:22b—It is contrasted with a faith perfected as a result of works.
> 2:24—It is a faith that is alone.
> 2:26—It is a faith without works that is dead.

This is also seen in James's usage of "believe" (a cognate of "faith"):

> 2:19a—It is assent to the unity of God.
> 2:19b—It is a kind of faith that even demons possess.
> 2:23—It is contrasted with the type of faith possessed by Abraham.[13]

13. Ibid.

It is clear that we must distinguish between faith as under- stood by James and the kind of faith envisioned by his opponent. James considers this opposing view of faith to be bogus. True faith includes intellectual assent to truths, but also includes personal trust, manifests itself in obedience to God, and displays mercy toward others.

James's view of genuine faith actually resembles Paul's very closely. For Paul, faith is a wholehearted trust in Christ for salvation.[14] Faith in Christ is not merely belief in truths about Christ, but is relational and includes personal commitment to Jesus and his ways. Justification is by faith and leads to a life of obedience. To claim faith in Jesus while retaining a life of sin is vehemently attacked by Paul (Rom. 6:1), who himself speaks of "the obedience of faith" (Rom. 1:5) and the necessity of "faith working through love" (Gal. 5:6).

That James is not responding to a truly Pauline understanding of faith is seen in his usage of "faith" *and* his usage of "works." James mentions "works" fifteen times—twelve times in 2:14–26 and three other times (1:4, linked with endurance; 1:25, linked with doing the word; and 3:13, linked with good fruits of wisdom). Stein concludes: "It should be noted that in 2:14–26, and in the rest of James, 'works' are always seen positively and, when described, involve acts of loving mercy, kindness, and obedience to God. . . . They have nothing to do with ritualistic or ceremonial actions."[15]

Paul does not use "works" in this way. When Paul uses some form of "works" in conjunction with his teachings related to justification, he contrasts them with faith and grace. For Paul in that context, "works" typically refer to trying to gain a right standing before God. Used in this way, these "works" are not justifying (Rom. 3:20), seek to make God a debtor in giving salvation (Rom. 4:2), and undermine the gracious nature of salvation (Rom. 11:6).[16] Sometimes Paul also refers to the "works of the law" and in doing so often refers to circumcision, Sabbath keeping, food laws, and other ritualistic and ceremonial laws. Opposing the Judaizers, Paul

14. Ibid.
15. Ibid., 7.
16. Ibid.

maintains that Gentiles can become Christians apart from performing these Jewish ceremonies and keeping Jewish regulations. Thus, Paul critiques "works" when he argues that salvation is based on the grace of God and the saving work of Christ. We receive salvation as a gift from God, through faith, not because of our works. But Paul also teaches that salvation produces good works. It is helpful to note Paul's view of works in Ephesians 2:8–10: "For by grace you have been saved through faith. And this is not your own doing; it is the gift of God, not a result of works, so that no one may boast. For we are his workmanship, created in Christ Jesus for good works, which God prepared beforehand, that we should walk in them." Notice the two ways in which "works" work in this passage. First, doing good works is not the way to receive salvation. Salvation is by grace through faith, is not based on our efforts, and is not a result of our works. Yet salvation issues in "good works," which are indicative of Christian living and are eternally planned by God. So, for Paul, are good works necessary in salvation? Yes and no. They are not the means of receiving salvation. God graciously gives salvation through faith. Yet true faith issues in good works, love, good fruit, and obedience to Christ. Such works are not additives to faith, but organic expressions of genuine faith.

Using similar evidence, Peter Davids maintains that James and Paul are writing on different subjects:

> Paul is justifying the reception of Gentiles into the church without circumcision whereas James is discussing the problem of the failure of works of charity within the church (which may be totally Jewish). If James intends to contradict Paul, he has so misunderstood him that his use of biblical citations and the meanings of similar expressions are totally different. This would hardly indicate he had read Romans.[17]

The apparent verbal similarity between Paul and James does not involve similar uses of the terms themselves, so it is

17. Peter H. Davids, *The Epistle of James*, New International Greek Testament Commentary (Grand Rapids: Eerdmans, 1982), 131.

unnecessary to posit that James writes in response to Paul or to a distortion of his teaching. But the careful reader may ask: what about the appeal to Abraham in both accounts? Richard Bauckham helpfully addresses this question at length. He explains, "That James uses the example of Abraham to prove his point is not surprising but virtually predictable, since for Second Temple Judaism Abraham was *par excellence* the exemplar of faith in God."[18] Bauckham continues: "God had already declared Abraham righteous on account of his faith in Genesis 15:6, but this verdict was confirmed when his faith is tested and proves itself in Genesis 22."[19] Bauckham concludes:

> James's account of Abraham's faith and works would closely follow established Jewish interpretation, adopting key terminology already used in that discussion, which James only needs to apply to the particular issue he addresses. Paul would be dependent on the same Jewish exegetical tradition with reference to Abraham, but more creatively adopts the terminology to make a different point: that Abraham was already justified by faith in the promise before he obeyed the commandment of circumcision and became the forerunner of specifically Jewish works. This hypothesis, that James and Paul are both continuing, in their different ways, a Jewish exegetical discussion of Abraham's faith, accounts for the parallels and differences between them more satisfactorily than postulating a direct relationship between them.[20]

Bauckham's case is persuasive. It seems then that the "James without reference to Paul" view is the most compelling response to the historical question.

The question then follows: to what is James responding? One promising answer to this question might be that James is expanding on the thought begun in 2:1–13. Thus, James would be warning believers not to court the wealthy or give credibility to the faith of the rich who are in their community. James would

18. Bauckham, *James*, 122.
19. Ibid., 123.
20. Ibid., 131.

be giving a caution: the rich (and others) who offer empty words to oppressed Christians without also meeting their tangible needs are displaying a lack of love, and therefore a lack of faith. True faith produces good works—which James especially characterizes as deeds of mercy. This makes sense of Abraham and Rahab, who are depicted as generous people.[21]

Another strong possibility is that James is simply continuing his overall call for consistency in the church and the Christian life. He would be addressing a practical heresy. Bauckham posits the following scenario:

> [W]e need only suppose that James was aware of the danger that some of his readers, complacently priding themselves on their monotheistic belief, neglected practical works of charity. They need not have professed the doctrinal view that their faith was sufficient to justify them, but they behaved as though this were the case. So James voices for them the theological claim that could express their attitude and behavior in order to show them that these cannot be defended.[22]

Thus, the context would be understood more broadly and as essentially the same as that of the rest of James. Such a practical heresy is perennial—people often fail to live out what they claim to believe. The Old Testament law, history, prophets, and wisdom literature all frequently address this common concern. Jesus targeted this recurrent problem as well (e.g., Matt. 25:31–46). This hypothesis best fits the evidence in James, as we will see below.

The Theological Question: What Does James 2:14–26 Teach?

Seeing James 2:14–26 in the context of James's previous argument is critical.[23] James 1 exhorts readers to be doers of the word

21. Davids, *James*, 132–33, observes that Jewish tradition regards Abraham and Rahab as examples of charity.
22. Bauckham, *James*, 125–26.
23. Tim Laato, "Justification according to James: A Comparison with Paul," *Trinity Journal* 18 (1997): 43–84.

and not to be deceived by a religion that does not lead to control over one's speech or to giving help to widows and orphans. James 2:1–13 applies that exhortation to the sin of showing favoritism, points to love as central to keeping the law, and declares that God will show no mercy to those who show no mercy to others. James 3:1–18 follows this section and stresses consistency in speech and lifestyle as prerequisite for all who aspire to be teachers in the church.

In 2:14–26, in memorable style and with powerful argumentation, James shows what genuine faith and wisdom are: they go beyond the empty recitation of religious words and express themselves in tangible acts of obedience. He insists that genuine saving faith results in good works (with deeds of mercy especially in view). Ten times in this paragraph, faith and works are mentioned together. Faith and works are not enemies of one another—not at all. Rather, righteous works authenticate genuine faith and display Christian consistency.

James 2:14 begins this section by asking two rhetorical questions. "What good is it," James asks, "if someone says he has faith but does not have works?" His imagined interlocutor claims to have genuine faith. Yet if his life is characterized by words without deeds, "can that faith save him?"

The illustration in James 2:15–16 unfolds the argument by drawing a scene in which fellow believers are in need of basic necessities, such as food and clothes. Yet instead of receiving tangible help, they are only given a verbal blessing: "Go in peace, be warmed and be filled" (2:16). Needs are left unmet; only words are offered. James reasons, "So also faith by itself, if it does not have works, is dead" (2:17). As long as religious people fail to minister to the needs of people they encounter, they are no better than the priest and the Levite in Jesus' parable of the good Samaritan (Luke 10:25–37). Such religion is not faithful but hypocritical. True Christianity results in love for others.

The argument develops as James anticipates another objection: "But someone will say, 'You have faith and I have works'" (2:18). James retorts that living faith cannot be separated from

138

deeds and challenges the hypothetical objector to show his faith in a tangible way (cf. 3:13; Matt. 7:16–17). Faith without works is orthodox in content, but dead in practice. It is useless to quote the Shema, "God is one" (2:19; cf. Deut. 6:4), but fail to carry out its interwoven requirement: "You shall love the LORD your God with all your heart and with all your soul and with all your might" (Deut. 6:5). James sarcastically jibes: "You do well. Even the demons believe—and shudder!" (2:19). How ridiculous it is for people to state their belief in God, as required by Deuteronomy 6:4, without manifesting love and obedience to God, as prescribed in Deuteronomy 6:5. Such religion is a sham. Genuine faith results in genuine works; to deny that is the height of foolishness (2:20).

Having illustrated the absurdity of inconsistent religion, James shifts his argument to demonstrate that Scripture teaches that obedience flows from true faith. As examples of faith, works, and mercy, James points to Abraham and Rahab—a patriarch and a prostitute, a Jew and a Gentile.[24] Here James uses the terminology of justification differently than Paul normally does. As the context of 2:12–13 makes clear, James teaches that if our faith is demonstrated in our works, we will be judged and found righteous. James is not saying that justification in the Pauline sense of the word is by works. Rather, our final judgment is according to works. This is the teaching of Jesus (Matt. 7:21–23, 24–27; 12:36; 16:27; 25:31–46), Peter (1 Peter 1:17), John (Rev. 20:12–15; 22:12), and even Paul (Rom. 2:1–16; 2 Cor. 5:9–10). As we previously said, works do not earn one a righteous standing before God. Yet God's grace that leads to initial faith also brings about continued faith, which is tied to covenant faithfulness. This is sometimes called good works, the obedience of faith, deeds of love, and the fruit of the Spirit.[25] Although the terminology varies, the idea is the same: believers' good works are rooted in faith, which flows from being

24. Mark Proctor, "Faith, Works, and the Christian Religion in James 2:14–26," *Evangelical Quarterly* 69, no. 4 (1997): 322–31.

25. James and Paul use strikingly different terminology as it relates to works. In Galatians 5:16–25, Paul contrasts works with the fruit of the Spirit. In James 2:14–26 and 3:13–18, we see characteristics that resemble Paul's list of fruit as indicative of true faith and wisdom.

brought forth by God as a new creation (James 1:18)—which, Paul and John underscore, comes through union with Christ and his saving work. John Calvin marvelously explains the relationship between new life, faith, and works:

> Although we may distinguish them [justification and sanctification], Christ contains both of them inseparably in himself. Do you wish, then, to attain righteousness in Christ? You must first possess Christ; but you cannot possess him without being made a partaker in his sanctification, because he cannot be divided into pieces [1 Cor. 1:13]. Since, therefore, it is solely by expending himself that the Lord gives us these benefits to enjoy, he bestows both of them at the same time, the one never without the other. Thus it is clear how true it is that we are justified not without works yet not through works, since in our sharing in Christ, which justifies us, sanctification is just as much included as righteousness.[26]

Through the example of Abraham, James emphasizes that faith is always accompanied by works (2:21), is active alongside works (2:22), and is completed by works (2:22), which is tied to Abraham's being counted by God as righteous and being called a friend of God (2:23). James then reiterates his conclusion that only people whose faith displays works are bona fide followers of God. Their consistency shows their genuineness (2:24). Jonathan Edwards similarly states:

> The drift of the apostle does not require that he should be understood in any other sense; for all that he aims at, as appears by a view of the context, is to prove that good works are necessary. The error of those that he opposed was this: that good works were not necessary to salvation, that if they did but believe that there was but one God, and that Christ was the Son of God and the like, and were baptized, they were safe, let them live how they would, which doctrine greatly tended

---

26. John Calvin, *Institutes of the Christian Religion*, ed. John T. McNeill, trans. Ford Lewis Battles (Philadelphia: Westminster Press, 1960), 3.16.1.

to licentiousness. The evincing the contrary of this is evidently the apostle's scope.[27]

John Calvin put it memorably: "Faith alone justifies, but faith that justifies is never alone."[28]

Through the example of Rahab, James makes the same point (2:25). Despite her original vocation as a prostitute, she became a heroine of faith in Jewish tradition. Rahab's faith is portrayed in Joshua 2:11 and confirmed in Hebrews 11:31. She acted on that faith, harboring the Jewish spies who came to her city and sending them out safely. Her deeds of love and commitment displayed her heart of faith.

James brings his argument to a close: "For as the body apart from the spirit is dead, so also faith apart from works is dead" (2:26). Creed and conduct cannot be separated any more than the body from air. Without air, the body is a corpse. Without works, faith is dead. Religious words without accompanying works of love are worthless.

Tim Laato summarizes well the basic arguments related to faith and works in James 2:14–26:

1. Faith without works is dead (2:17, 26).
2. Faith itself (not merely the believer) has works (2:17).
3. More broadly, faith without works works nothing (2:20).
4. The faith of Abraham worked with his works (2:22).
5. The faith of Abraham was completed by works (2:22).

Regarding the fifth point, Laato explains that works do not supplement faith, but that works in a certain sense realize the essence of faith.[29]

James thus teaches that true faith includes intellectual assent to truths and also includes personal trust. Even more, true faith

27. Jonathan Edwards, "Justification by Faith Alone," in *The Works of Jonathan Edwards*, ed. Edward Hickman, 2 vols. (Edinburgh: Banner of Truth Trust, 1974), 1:651.

28. Cf. John Calvin, *Commentaries on the Catholic Epistles*, trans. John Owen, Calvin's Commentaries (repr., Grand Rapids: Baker, 1979), 309–17.

29. Laato, "Justification according to James," 62–63.

manifests itself in obedience to God as well as in acts of mercy toward others. Orthodox theology is necessary, but not sufficient. Genuine followers of Christ hear the word and do it. They not only claim to have faith, but reflect it in their walk with God and their deeds of love.

The Canonical Question: Are the Teachings of James and Paul Compatible?

The answer to this question falls into place, now that the historical and theological questions have been addressed: James and Paul are not inconsistent. As Thomas Schreiner states:

> James does not disagree with Paul's contention that faith alone justifies, but he defines carefully the kind of faith that justifies. The faith that truly justifies can never be separated from works. Works will inevitably flow as the fruit of such faith. . . . The faith that saves is living, active, and dynamic. It must produce works, just as compassion for the poor inevitably means that one cares practically for their physical needs (James 2:15–16).[30]

While using similar terms, James and Paul speak to distinct theological and pastoral problems in diverse contexts. James and Paul have different emphases, and seem to use the faith of Abraham and the data somewhat differently.[31] Despite this, they reflect an overall theological and pastoral consistency.

Both messages need to be heard today. When we are tempted to assume that we are Christians, but rarely follow Christ's commands, James reminds us that true faith results in obeying God and loving others. When we are tempted to suppose that we contribute to our salvation by what we do, Paul reminds us that salvation is through the saving work of Christ, by grace alone,

---

30. Thomas R. Schreiner, *New Testament Theology: Magnifying God in Christ* (Grand Rapids: Baker, 2008), 604.

31. D. A. Carson, "James," in *Commentary on the New Testament Use of the Old Testament*, ed. D. A. Carson and G. K. Beale (Grand Rapids: Baker, 2007), 1005.

142

and received by faith alone. Thus, when speaking of justification and works, Paul typically cautions us to remember that we are saved by God's grace and not because of anything we contribute; using similar language, James tells us that true Christians follow Christ's teachings and love others.

It is important to note that both James and Paul share much in common in relation to the doctrine of salvation. Both teach that salvation is grounded in God's sovereign election (James 2:5–7; Eph. 1:3–14), that the new creation comes from God's gracious initiative (James 1:18; Eph. 2:4–7), that salvation is linked to the effective power of the gospel (James 1:18; Eph. 1:13; Rom. 1:16), that genuine faith is necessary (James 2:14–26; Eph. 2:8–10), that works of love and obedience are the inevitable consequence of genuine faith (James 2:14–26; Eph. 2:10), and that the final judgment is according to works (James 2:12–26; Rom. 2:6–15). Although the teachings of Paul and James stress different truths, their doctrines of salvation are quite compatible.

11

A Sketch of James's Theology

BEFORE WE EXAMININE the particulars of James's theology, some preliminary considerations and personal conclusions are in order. First, James has a theology, and it is foundational to the letter. Although he teaches little that would have been considered groundbreaking to Jewish Christians in the first century, he integrates the Old Testament and the teachings of Jesus in a way that sheds light on the beliefs of the earliest Jewish-Christian churches. James forcefully calls these communities to live in a way that is consistent with their theology. As we will see in the next chapter, "Theology at Work," James often bases his exhortations for Christian living on his theology, particularly his doctrines of God, the church, and last things.

Second, a full-blown theology of James cannot be discovered in this letter, for it is written by an insider to insiders, with much being assumed. In a way, reading any New Testament letter is like listening to one side of a phone conversation. We know what is being said on that one side, but we do not know what may have shaped the choice of words and emphases. Trying to recover a developed theology in such a brief and occasional letter would seem to be unrealistic. Plus, James did not write this letter to expand the church's theology, but to address particular concerns that Christians faced. So while I am more optimistic than many that James's theology is integrated into the letter and

145

can be somewhat known, I am more pessimistic than some who strive to discover a full-orbed theology of James. With too little material to know his overall theological system, but with enough to discover aspects of his theology, I suggest we work *toward* a theology of James.

We began by looking at the story of James and then addressed the influences on his thought, highlighted his primary burden, and unpacked his major themes. Now we examine James's primary theological teachings on God, humanity, sin, Jesus, salvation, the Christian life, the church, and last things.[1] Our goal is to sketch briefly the contours of James's theology.[2]

- God
- Jesus
- The Holy Spirit
- Humanity and Sin
- Salvation and the Christian Life
- The Church
- Last Things

God

James is a God-saturated work. Just look at the references to God in this brief epistle:

1:1—God as master (James as "servant of God")
1:5—God as the generous giver of wisdom
1:13—God as holy ("cannot be tempted" and "tempts no one")
1:17—God as transcendent ("from above")
1:17—God as the source of every good and perfect gift

1. The topic of revelation and Scripture was addressed previously, so it will not be repeated here.
2. Reading John W. Mahony, "The Origin of Jacobean Thought" (PhD diss., Mid-America Baptist Theological Seminary, 1982), 79–169, opened my eyes to James's robust theology and stimulated several ideas in this chapter.

1:17—God as "the Father of lights"

1:17—God as unchangingly good ("no variation or shadow due to change")

1:18—God as Savior and Re-creator ("he brought us forth by the word of truth")

1:18—God as Creator ("of his creation")

2:5—God as choosing the poor to be rich in faith

2:5—God as promising the kingdom to those who love him

2:12—God as Lawgiver and Judge

2:19—God as one (monotheism)

2:23—God as the proper object of faith

2:23—God as a friend of Abraham and all true believers

3:9—God as worthy of blessing

3:9—God as the creator of humans in his image

4:4—God as jealous and wrathful

4:6—God as gracious

4:8—God as personal

4:8—God as demanding moral purity

4:12—God as Lawgiver and Judge

4:15—God as the sovereign king (controlling history according to his will)

5:1—God as the avenger of his people

5:1—God as punishing the wicked

5:4—God as knowing our actions

5:4—God as Lord of armies, the warrior

5:8—God as bringing the final consummation of history

5:11—God as purposeful

5:11—God as merciful and compassionate

5:15—God as the healer of the sick

5:16—God as answering prayer

5:20—God as the one who forgives sins

James's doctrine of God is more substantial than is often recognized. In only five chapters, James speaks of many divine attributes. From the outset, James depicts God as the wise giver of wisdom (1:2–8), who is generous in his giving (1:5) and faithful to his promises, blessing those who persevere (1:12). God is utterly good, transcendent, and consistent (1:13–17). He does not seek to trip up his people, but is for them and blesses them with every good and perfect gift. God is righteous and expects his people to reflect his character (1:20); he is holy and demands unstained living (1:27). God is one, as Deuteronomy 6:4–7 declares (2:19). Furthermore, he is jealous like a husband (4:4–5), yet gracious to the humble (4:6) and drawing near to receive worship from his submissive people (4:8). He is also sovereign, the one in control of history, the one to whom we submit all of our plans (4:15). The good, just, and wrathful God also sees and knows all things happening against his people, and he will vindicate them and punish the wicked (5:1–6). Thankfully, as Exodus 34:6–7 shows, God is compassionate and merciful to his people, displaying covenant faithfulness (5:11).

James refers to God with various designations. The most familiar include God, Father, and Lord. God is also both the Judge and the Lawgiver (2:8–13; 4:11–12). This depiction of God as Lawgiver and Judge, along with his ability to save and destroy, may point both back to the Exodus-Sinai event and forward to the last judgment.[3] In any case, God not only reveals his covenant commands, but also judges according to them. As the Lord of hosts, the warrior, he also enforces them (5:1–11). God is also like a husband who demands that his people (pictured as a wife) remain faithful to him (note the adultery motif in 4:4–6). One unusual depiction of God is as "the Father of lights" (1:16–18). The idea seems to be that God, as the creator of the heavenly bodies, does not change as the heavenly lights do.[4] These created entities vary, but God remains the same. As Thomas Schreiner states, "His goodness is reflected in both the old creation and the new creation."[5] This

3. William Brosend II, *James and Jude*, New Cambridge Bible Commentary (Cambridge: Cambridge University Press, 2004), 120–22.

4. See Esther Yue L. Ng, "Father-God Language and Old Testament Allusions in James," *Tyndale Bulletin* 54, no. 2 (2003): 41–54.

5. Thomas R. Schreiner, *New Testament Theology: Magnifying God in Christ* (Grand Rapids: Baker, 2008), 153.

idea of God's goodness, stability, and integrity recurs in James as he appeals to his readers to reflect that integrity.

James also depicts God's works in his epistle. God gives wisdom (1:2–5; 3:13–18), humbles the rich (1:9–11), exalts the poor (1:9–11), rewards perseverance (1:12), gives every good gift (1:16–17), bestows new life (1:18), and creates (1:18). He also defines and accepts proper religion and worship (1:25–27; 4:4–10), chooses the poor (2:4–7), promises a kingdom (2:4–7), gives the law (2:8–13), judges according to it (2:8–13), is the proper object of faith (2:14–26), and is a friend of Abraham (2:20–26). Even more, God creates humans in his image (3:9–12), opposes the proud (4:1–10), exalts the humble (4:1–10), has authority to save or destroy (4:11–12), providentially guides history (4:13–17; cf. 1:13–18), defends the poor (5:1–6), avenges his people (5:1–11), defeats the wicked (5:1–6), knows human actions (5:1–11), will consummate history through Jesus' return (5:7–11), heals the sick (5:13–16), answers prayer (1:5; 4:3; 5:14–18), and forgives sin (5:19–20). In sum, God's works include creation, providence, salvation, miracles, and judgment.

It is striking how much James's doctrine of God is rooted in the Old Testament. Some texts, like James 4:6, are clear echoes: God opposes the proud and gives grace to the humble (cf. Prov. 3:34). James 5:11 is another example: God is compassionate and merciful (cf. Ex. 34:6–7). Other passages are more thematic and provide overall perspectives: God is one, personal, the judge, a warrior, and the source of wisdom.

James's doctrine of God also reflects the teachings of Jesus.[6] G. B. Stevens said that in James "we see the God of the Old Covenant clothed in qualities which distinguish Jesus' conception of the Father in Heaven."[7] Some of these conceptions of God are linked closely to Jesus, such as James 4:12: God is able to save and destroy (cf. Matt. 10:28). Others are more broadly connected,

6. The way James uses Jesus' kingdom teachings for existing churches undercuts views that the Sermon on the Mount should be interpreted as a utopian ideal or a future millennial ethic.

7. George Barker Stevens, *The Theology of the New Testament* (Edinburgh: T & T Clark, 1918), 277. I owe this quote to Mahony, "The Origin of Jacobean Thought," 79–80.

such as God forgiving sin, answering prayer, healing in connection with faith and his name, and choosing the poor.

As we will see in the next chapter, the doctrine of God is central to James's ethical exhortations.

Jesus

> The book [James] has become better known for its omissions than its affirmations. . . . To be sure, what is not (apparently) in the book of James may be at first striking. There is no mention of the cross . . . the resurrection, the gift of the Spirit, or baptism and the Lord's Supper. Most noticeable perhaps among the omissions in this New Testament book are frequent references to Jesus and His Christological titles.[8]

Robert Sloan rightly brings the question to the forefront: what does James actually teach about Jesus?

Three strands of data stand out. First are the teachings of Jesus. Through his use of Jesus' teachings, James displays his view of Jesus' authority. James reinterprets God's word and law in light of Jesus as the eschatological bearer of the new covenant. As we saw previously, Jesus' teaching inspires many of James's instructions and shapes his handling of passages like Leviticus 19 and Exodus 20. Thus, in the teachings of James, Jesus is an authoritative teacher, whose words are on par with the Old Testament.

The second strand of data includes the teachings that are clearly about Jesus. The epistle begins, "James, a servant of God and of the Lord Jesus Christ" (1:1). James immediately speaks of himself as a bond servant to God and Jesus, which implies that they both have the same status and authority. This is shocking language for a Jewish monotheist.[9] James here also represents Jesus as the Christ, which in context would connote the eschatological Messiah, the promised Davidic king, the fulfillment

8. Robert B. Sloan, "The Christology of James," *Criswell Theological Review* 1, no. 1 (1986): 3.
9. Schreiner, *New Testament Theology*, 400–401.

of the Old Testament hope. Plus, he depicts him as "Lord" (cf. 2:1; 5:7, 9). William Baker observes: "The significance of James applying to Jesus the Septuagintal word for Yahweh who covenanted with Israel cannot be overstated. Yet, in doing this, James parallels what must have become common practice among early Christians, since calling Jesus as 'Lord' is commonplace in the New Testament."[10]

Another key passage is James 2:1, where the word "glory" is used in connection with Jesus. Considerable discussion has arisen as to what exactly James is saying. Three views stand out. First, some propose that 2:1 should read "our Lord Jesus Christ, the glory."[11] According to this view, "glory" is a euphemism for God, much like what we find in 2 Peter 1:17, where God the Father is called "the Majestic Glory." Second, some render it, as does the English Standard Version, "our Lord Jesus Christ, the Lord of glory." Here Jesus is not "the glory," but rather, as in 1 Corinthians 2:8, "the Lord of glory," which is reminiscent of "the King of glory" in Psalm 24:7–10.[12] Third, some translate it, as does the New International Version, "our glorious Lord Jesus Christ." Here "glory" is understood as an adjective describing Jesus.[13] While the exact meaning of the passage remains uncertain, the overarching theological truth is clear and magnificent: Jesus is glorious! For those steeped in Judaism to declare Jesus "glorious," "the glory," or "the Lord of glory" testifies to belief in his deity. This also probably refers to his resurrection, as "Lord" and "glory" are often used in resurrection contexts (cf. 2 Cor. 4:5; Phil. 2:6–11). "Glory" has a range of meanings in Scripture and is often associated with God's covenant presence and name (cf. 2:5), as well as the display of his holiness, power, victory, judgment, and more.

---

10. William R. Baker, "Christology in the Epistle of James," *Evangelical Quarterly* 74, no. 1 (2002): 53.

11. Sloan, "The Christology of James," 21; cf. P. J. Townsend, "Christ, Community, and Salvation in the Epistle of James," *Evangelical Quarterly* 53 (1981): 116.

12. Richard Bauckham, *James: Wisdom of James, Disciple of Jesus the Sage* (London: Routledge, 1999), 139, notes that James 4:8 also alludes to Psalm 24:3–4.

13. Richard R. Melick Jr., "The Glory of God in the Synoptic Gospels, Acts, and General Epistles," in *The Glory of God*, ed. Christopher W. Morgan and Robert A. Peterson, Theology in Community (Wheaton, IL: Crossway, 2010).

Jesus is further depicted as the one who is being blasphemed by the oppressive, exploitive landowners in 2:1–7.[14] James 2:7 reads, "Are they not the ones who blaspheme the honorable name by which you were called?" In view of Jesus' teachings elsewhere (e.g., Matt. 25:31–46), this "name" is that of Jesus. Jewish Christians no doubt understood this in light of the theological use of "the name" in the Old Testament (cf. Lev. 19:11–12). Reminiscent of Deuteronomy 28:10 ("You are called by the name of the LORD"; cf. Isa. 43:7; Jer. 14:9; Amos 9:12), James 2:7 links Jesus with Yahweh himself. Incredibly, the people of God are now the people of Jesus, called by Jesus and identified with Jesus. They bear his name; their identity is in him. To persecute the people of God is therefore to persecute Jesus, as Paul found in Acts 9:5. This understanding surfaces again in James 5:14, in which the sick are anointed "in the name of the Lord." James, like many other witnesses in the New Testament, points to healing and other miracles done by Christians in the name of the Lord (see Acts 3:6; 4:30; 16:18). James adds: "And the Lord will raise him up. And if he has committed sins, he will be forgiven" (5:15). The sick also appear to be raised up by Jesus himself. The juxtaposition of the forgiveness with the healing also makes it plausible that Jesus is understood as the forgiver. Jesus is active, present, and powerful in and through the church.[15]

While Jesus is currently present in and through the church, the full manifestation of his presence remains in the future. James speaks of the nearness of "the coming of the Lord" (5:7, 9), which refers to Jesus, reflects Jesus' own teaching (Matt. 24:3, 32), and is found elsewhere in the New Testament (cf. 1 Cor. 15:23–24; 1 Thess. 3:13; Rev. 3:20). This coming is linked to victory over, and the judgment of, evil; "the Judge is standing at the door" (James 5:9; cf. Matt. 24:33). Baker reasons:

After the monotheistic pronouncement about God put into the mouths of demons in 2:19, it is difficult to think that anyone but

14. Peter H. Davids, *The Epistle of James*, New International Greek Testament Commentary (Grand Rapids: Eerdmans, 1982), 113, considers this certain.
15. Baker, "Christology in the Epistle of James," 56.

God is in mind here, even though the "law" which he depicts God as assessing in believers is judging "your neighbor." However, despite James's pronouncement that there is only one Judge, it appears to most that he applies the term Judge to Christ just a few verses later in 5:9. In a context of awaiting the "Lord's coming," an idea which dominates New Testament ideas about Christ, and speaking of this Judge "standing at the door," a picture also drawn of Christ in Matthew 24:32, Mark 13:29, and Revelation 3:20, it is difficult to avoid understanding James to refer to anyone other than Christ.[16]

If this interpretation is right, James teaches that Jesus is the coming Lord, the Judge, and thus the consummator of redemptive history. The Old Testament prophets refer to this eschatological scenario of judgment and deliverance as "the day of Yahweh." James ties this long-anticipated day to Jesus' coming and judgment; the day of Yahweh is now the day of Christ (cf. Phil. 1:10).

This leads to the third strand of Christological material: teachings of James that might be about Jesus. Sloan argues that since Jesus is the Judge in 5:9, and there is only one God (2:19) and only one Judge (4:11–12), James has Jesus in view as the Judge in 4:11–12. If this is so, then Jesus would necessarily be identified as the Lawgiver depicted in 4:11–12.[17] Others suggest that James uses the titles more broadly to refer to God. This seems more likely, since God is the clear referent in 4:4–9 and the likely referent in 4:10 and 4:13–16.

There are other passages in which James refers to the "Lord" without giving enough detail to specify whether Jesus is in view. James 4:10 is such a case, though it is hard not to see the general reference to God here. James 4:4–9 is linked to God, and 4:11–12 and 4:13–16 seem to be as well. Another case in point is "if the Lord wills" (4:15). "Lord" here could arguably refer to Jesus, as

---

16. Ibid., 54–55. Others who agree include Sloan, "The Christology of James," 23–27; Davids, *James*, 185; Ralph P. Martin, *James*, Word Biblical Commentary (Waco, TX: Word, 1988), 162; Douglas J. Moo, *The Letter of James*, Pillar New Testament Commentary (Grand Rapids: Eerdmans, 2000), 225.

17. Sloan, "The Christology of James," 23–27.

Larry Hurtado takes it.[18] Or it could be understood more generally, as Baker interprets it.[19] The same question emerges in 5:10, "the prophets who spoke in the name of the Lord," and 5:11, "the purpose of the Lord, how the Lord is compassionate and merciful." The reference to the prophets and the allusion to Exodus 34:6–7 suggest that the broader conception of God is in view.

A more likely teaching about Jesus is found in James 2:1. Depending on how one takes the genitive construction in 2:1 (literally, "the faith *of* our Lord Jesus Christ"), James teaches that Jesus is either the object of faith or the (example of) one who has faith. The context and the grammar are not definitive, so, as we would expect, scholars disagree on this—and often along theological lines. Protestant and Reformed scholars like Peter Davids, Douglas Moo, and Thomas Schreiner suggest that this means "faith in Jesus," which results in the theological truth that Jesus is the object of our faith. Roman Catholic scholars like Luke Johnson propose "the faith of Jesus," which highlights the example of Jesus and his faithfulness.[20] The first would understand James 2:1 as "do not show favoritism because it is inconsistent with genuine faith in Christ." The second would see it as "do not show favoritism because it is inconsistent with the example of Christ." I prefer the former, primarily because I think it best fits the emphasis on consistent and integrated faith that precedes and follows it (1:26–27; 2:14–26). If so, then James teaches that Jesus is the object of our faith.

Putting all this together, we find that far from having a low or nonexistent Christology,[21] James, for a letter composed at such an early date, actually displays a remarkably high Christology (though

---

18. Larry W. Hurtado, "Christology," in *Dictionary of the Later New Testament and Its Developments*, ed. Ralph P. Martin and Peter H. Davids (Downers Grove, IL: InterVarsity Press, 1997), 173.

19. Baker, "Christology in the Epistle of James," 54–55.

20. Davids, *James*, 182; Moo, *James*, PNTC, 100–101; Schreiner, *New Testament Theology*, 402; Luke Timothy Johnson, *The Letter of James*, The Anchor Bible (New York: Doubleday, 1995), 220.

21. For an example of such a view, see Martin Dibelius, *A Commentary on the Epistle of James*, rev. Heinrich Greeven, Hermeneia Commentary (Philadelphia: Fortress, 1976), 66, 126–28.

not as developed as that of Paul, John, and so on). Bauckham is right: "Christology, though presumed more than expounded, is more prominent and considerably higher than is often allowed."[22] Jesus is the authoritative teacher, the revealer of truth, and the eschatological Messiah. He is also the Lord, characterized by glory, the one who has called to himself a people by his name, and the one who heals in his name. He is the coming Lord and Judge, the one who comes and judges on the day of Yahweh, bringing final punishment upon the wicked, final salvation to his people, and ultimate victory to the cosmos.

In James's portrait, Jesus is depicted as divine, yet as distinct from God. From the beginning verse, James displays this theological tension, "James, a servant of God and of the Lord Jesus Christ" (1:1). Yet the particularities of this relationship are not spelled out. Terms like "Lord" are used both generally for God and also for Jesus. Both are identified as Judge, yet James points to the reality of only one Judge and Lawgiver. So, there is one God (2:19), who is the Judge (4:11–12), but Jesus is also the Judge, and, as we just saw, he is "associated with God in astonishing ways."[23] Jesus bears divine titles (Lord), divine uniqueness (name), divine attributes (glory), and divine prerogatives and roles (eschatological consummation, judgment, and the object of our faith). Yet he is distinguished from God. Thus, even in this very early period of the church, we find five truths that could be characterized as part of a Trinitarian trajectory: God is one, the Father is God, Jesus is divine, the Father and Jesus are distinct, and the Father and Jesus exist in unity.

The Holy Spirit

Another point that has troubled scholars is that James makes no clear mention of the Holy Spirit. The New American Standard Bible and the Holman Christian Standard Bible take 4:5 as

22. Bauckham, *James*, 138.
23. Hurtado, "Christology," 178.

referring to the Holy Spirit: "He jealously desires the Spirit which He has made to dwell in us" (NASB); "the Spirit He has caused to live in us yearns jealously" (HCSB). Most translations differ. The English Standard Version translates it, "He yearns jealously over the spirit that he has made to dwell in us." The New International Version reads, "The spirit he caused to live in us envies intensely." Both translations are possible. If James 4:5 does refer to the Holy Spirit (which I doubt), then James teaches that the Spirit is personal, holy, and indwells God's people. Such instruction is similar to other biblical teaching.

Some scholars also see a similarity between James's use of wisdom and how other biblical writers speak of the Spirit. For instance, they remind that in the Old Testament the Spirit grants wisdom to the people of God. They also see a possible link between James 1:5 and Luke 11:13, where the good gift that God gives to those who ask in faith is the Spirit. They find the fruit of wisdom from above (James 3:13–18) similar to the fruit of the Spirit (Gal. 5:22–23).[24] Yet James urges believers to ask for wisdom, and he surely does not completely equate such wisdom with the Spirit (1:5–8). At best, these attempts to interpret these passages as the Holy Spirit are uncertain.

This leaves us without any firm basis to determine James's theology of the Holy Spirit or how he envisions the relationship between the Father, Jesus, and the Spirit. For such truths, we will have to be content to look to other biblical writers.

Humanity and Sin

The epistle of James also has more to say about humanity and sin than most would think. For example, God created people (1:18), whose life passes away rather quickly (1:9–11; 4:13–17).

24. J. A. Kirk, "The Meaning of Wisdom in James: Examination of a Hypothesis," *New Testament Studies* 16 (1969): 24–38, argues along these lines. Davids, *James*, 51–56, follows some of Kirk's conclusions. For a recent argument to the contrary, see William R. Baker, "Searching for the Holy Spirit in James: Is Wisdom Equivalent?" *Tyndale Bulletin* 50, no. 2 (November 2008): 293–320.

They are created in the image of God, and in part this is why they must be treated with respect and love, rather than cursing and slander (3:9–12). As creatures in God's image, they are also responsible to God and will stand before his judgment (2:8–13; 4:11–12). James also has implications related to the unity and composition of the human person, as he mentions things like the body, the soul, the spirit, the heart, and an overall unity (cf. 1:13–18; 2:14–26; 3:9–18).

James teaches much about the doctrine of sin. He underscores that the holy God is not the source of sin; instead, sin comes from the human heart, from within (1:13–15). James also speaks of both "sin" and "sins," recognizing the internal nature of sin as well as the outward manifestations of this inward rebellion (1:13–15; 2:9; 4:8; 5:15–16). The utter foolishness and mystery of sin also come across as James expresses dismay at the inconsistency of people (3:9–12). Because of the unity of the law, sin is rebellion against the Lawgiver and results in a totality of guilt (2:9–10). Sin is depicted as missing the mark and transgressing the law (2:9–11), as taking the wrong action (1:13–15), and as failing to take the right action (4:17). Sin is also universal. James includes himself in his assertion that no one has tamed the tongue (3:2, 8). Even teachers and apostles like James still sin. Believers are to be consistent and are ultimately being perfected, but until the day of Christ, they continue to struggle against sin.[25]

James also draws attention to the process of temptation and sin. God never tempts anyone, but the external temptation entices the internal desire, and that lust leads to sin, and that sin to death (1:13–18; see also Prov. 5, 7). John Owen warns: sin deceives, entices, conceives, develops, and finishes with death.[26] Temptation masks the fact that sin is really a serial killer! The old adage reflects James's teaching: sin takes you farther than you want to

---

25. Schreiner, *New Testament Theology*, 540.
26. John Owen, "Indwelling Sin," in *Overcoming Sin and Temptation: Three Classic Works by John Owen*, ed. Kelly M. Kapic and Justin Taylor (Wheaton, IL: Crossway, 2006), 295–96.

go, keeps you longer than you want to stay, and costs you more than you want to pay.

Sin is foremost against God. It displays itself in various forms: a lack of faith (1:5–8), double-mindedness (1:8), pride (1:9–11; 4:6), lust (1:13–15), filthiness (1:21), wickedness (1:21), lack of obedience to the word (1:22–25), pollution from the world (1:27), self-seeking passions (4:1–3), friendship with the world (4:4), refusal to submit humbly to God (4:4–10), presumption (4:13–17), boastfully swearing oaths (5:12), and wandering from the truth (5:19–20).

Sin also hurts the church. Pride and refusal to submit to God result in many offenses against the covenant community. These include anger (1:20), filthiness (1:21), wickedness (1:21), destructive words (1:26; 3:1–12), partiality (2:1–7), judging others (2:4; 4:11–12), and failure to show love and mercy, especially to the poor (2:8–26). It is also seen in cursing people (3:10), jealousy (3:14), selfish ambition (3:14), boasting (3:5, 14; 4:13–17), lying (3:14), self-promoting prayer (4:1, 3), quarreling in the church (4:1), hatred and speech so vicious that it is called "murder" (4:2), covetousness (4:2), slander of the family of God (4:11), oppression and exploitation of the poor (5:1–6), and grumbling against the people of God (5:9).

Sin is serious and brings consequences. For instance, the rich will pass away like a flower (1:10). Indeed, sin always leads to death (1:15; 5:20). Sin brings guilt before God, condemnation under his law (2:9–10), and appropriate judgment (2:12–13; 5:12). Sin produces disorder in the church (3:16–4:4), damage to the individual (4:1–3), enmity with God (4:4), opposition from God (4:6), moral filth (4:8), and destruction (4:12). For the wicked, it leads to a just final punishment depicted as miserable and painful (5:1–6).

In addition, James mentions both demons and the devil. He uses the demons as an example of orthodox belief without genuine faith (2:19). But he also depicts the demons as the source of false wisdom and its rotten fruit in churches: pride, disorder, jealously, and selfish ambition (3:1–10; 3:13–18). The devil is the evil adversary, accuser, or slanderer, to be resisted. If resisted, the devil flees from the consistent and humble people of God (4:7).

Salvation and the Christian Life

James roots salvation in the sovereignty and grace of God. The poor are rich in faith, are heirs of the kingdom, and are to be treated with respect because God has elected them (2:5). Indeed, God gives grace to the humble and opposes the proud (4:6).

Believers are also brought forth into a new creation because of the will of God, through the word of truth, to be firstfruits of God's creation. This new life is a gift of the good and holy God. William Baker suggests, "James's Christian readers are being told that their birth into a new life is an extension of God's original purpose for creating humanity in the first place."[27] Whereas sin leads to death, God the good Creator, the Father of lights, brings us forth into a new creation and life (1:13–18).

Believers display the reality of this new creation through covenant faithfulness. They bear the fruit of wisdom, obey God's word, live in holiness, love the people of God, and show mercy to the needy. As we saw in the chapter on "James and Paul," true faith is active. It brings with it works of love and grace.

James also depicts several broad perspectives on salvation and the Christian life. He links salvation to the already-and-not-yet nature of the kingdom, and as such it is past, present, and future. We have been elected, have been brought forth as the new creation, are presently faithful to the covenant, are firstfruits of his new creation, and will ultimately be blessed and given final salvation. Faith, too, is tied both to the already and to the not yet. It is initial, is continual, and must persevere to receive ultimate blessing (1:12, 25; 2:12–13, 14–26; 5:7–11, 19–20). Believers are also on their way to maturity. Indeed, tri-

27. William R. Baker, "Who's Your Daddy? Gendered Birth Images in the Soteriology of the Epistle of James (1:14–15, 18, 21)," *Evangelical Quarterly* 79, no. 3 (2007): 204.

als are not good in themselves, but they are active agents in this process of maturing believers (1:2–4). Interestingly, James both demands this wholeness and perfection and displays an awareness that sin is deep-seated in the church and individual Christians. James again reflects the teachings of Jesus, about which G. E. Ladd comments:

> Even as the Kingdom has invaded the evil age to bring men in advance a partial but real experience of the blessings of the eschatological Kingdom, so is the righteousness of the Kingdom attainable, in part if not in perfection, in the present order. Ethics, like the Kingdom itself, stand in the tension between present realization and future eschatological perfection.[28]

James holds expectations high, keeps warnings urgent, and yet acknowledges the present reality that church members are prone to temptation and sin and thus exhorts them to be consistent and calls for confession and repentance. Like a loving pastor, he urges perseverance, even concluding his letter with a plea for the church to promote such continued faith (5:19–20).

God uses the word in the entire process of salvation. He brought us forth into a new creation through the word, and he implants the word in us, yet we are to receive it and obey it throughout our lives. The word reveals the will of the Lawgiver and actively and effectively brings about the new creation.

The Christian life is to be characterized by faith, humility, love, and mercy. And the Christian life is to be lived in the context of the covenant community, the church. The Christian life is life together, life in community with other believers.

The Church

James writes to real-life churches with real-life problems, and he offers them wisdom for consistency. He speaks directly

28. G. E. Ladd, *The Presence of the Future: The Eschatology of Biblical Realism* (Grand Rapids: Eerdmans, 1974), 292.

and indirectly about what churches are and what they are supposed to be.

James does not portray a perfect church. Those who believe that all the contemporary church needs to solve its problems is a return to the pristine state of the New Testament church will find themselves frustrated that those churches too were riddled with problems. A desire for such a return is right in that it recognizes the need to ground our ecclesiology in the New Testament. But it tends to forget that sin was a serious problem in the New Testament church. Indeed, the presence of such sins as hypocrisy, inconsistency, pride, division, self-promotion, slander, and failure to show mercy to the hurting was a major reason why James wrote this epistle.

But through his instructions and corrections to these sin-torn churches, we learn what James believed that the church should be. For example, we see that the church is to be a community of family-like relationships, where love and service mark the members (1:2). The term "brothers," which James often uses (1:2, 16; 2:1, 14; 3:1, 10; 4:11; 5:7, 9, 10, 12, 19), depicts the church as a family, where people love one another and are bound to one another. This family gathers to encourage one another in following Christ, which involves ministry to those whom society oppresses. The church is to help those who cannot help themselves, to value the poor, and to treat everyone with respect (1:26–27; 2:1–13).

The church is also to be characterized by holiness and truth (1:19–27; 3:1–4:10). It is to be a community where believers repent of sin, practice self-control, and display faith through good deeds. It is to be a community where teachers are carefully selected to ensure that the truth is not distorted through false teaching or inconsistent lifestyles. It is to be a community of the word—a community which God both creates and sanctifies through the word.

The church is also to be a community of unity, prayer, and restoration (3:2–4:10; 5:13–20), in which people refuse to be self-seeking, humbly recognize sin, and edify one another, rather than tear each other down. Far from a being a people of slander and self-promotion, the church is to be the people of Jesus, marked by prayer and self-giving. There are to be mutual prayer, confession, and accountability.

In addition, the church is to be a community of patience (5:1–12), as it is an eschatological covenant community that exists in the already and the not yet. It should display the arrival of the kingdom through its relationships to God, with one another, and to society. Yet it still longs for the final arrival of the kingdom in its faith, hope, patience, and perseverance. The church is an eschatological covenant community where people should view their suffering as temporary, remember that the ungodly will ultimately be punished, await God's final victory and judgment, and stand firm in the meantime.

For James, the church is the people of Jesus who together pursue and channel wholeness and completeness. It is an eschatological, covenantal, worshipping community of believers, where the truth is taught, love for one another is genuine, mercy to the poor is displayed, and restoration of wanderers is sought. It is God's new creation, exemplifying the arrival of the kingdom as the firstfruits of the way things should and will be (1:18). As the church maintains such covenant faithfulness, God deems its worship to be acceptable and pure (1:26–27).

Since the epistle of James likely dates in the late forties, this portrait is one of the earliest we have of Christian churches. This is evident in the terminology James uses. Douglas Moo's comments on James 2:1–7 are helpful:

> The scenario is a "meeting." The Greek word is *synagoge*, used widely by the Jews to denote the place where they met for worship, instruction, and encouragement in the faith. Some think James's use of the word here indicates that he was writing to Jewish Christians who were still attending Jewish synagogue meetings. . . . But James's qualification of this "synagogue" as "your synagogue" implies that Christians had control over the meetings. Another possibility, then, is to think that James uses the word in its more general sense, a

"gathering" or an "assembly." . . . Jewish Christians who had recently embraced Jesus as their Messiah would naturally carry over into their new covenant worship the terms and conventions familiar to them from their past experience— even as they began using more technical "Christian" terms as well (cf. "church" in 5:14).[29]

This church is somewhat akin to the people of God in the Old Testament (1:1), yet defined now as the true people of God (1:1), even the people of Jesus (2:1–5).[30] It is also an assembly (2:1–4), a body with members (3:6; 4:1), a family, and has an organizational structure.

Contrary to the claims of some, the earliest churches possessed organizational structure. In James, several parts of the structure can be ascertained. First, the early church had apostles, like James himself. The local congregations, like Jewish synagogues, also had teachers (3:1) and elders (5:13–16). Also included are the members of the body, the congregation of believers (3:6; 4:1).

How these particular parts related to one another is unclear. For example, the extent of James's authority is unknown, but was real nevertheless. James, other apostles, the Jerusalem church, and other churches made pivotal decisions at key junctures in the church's history (Acts 15). Yet there is no evidence that James, unlike Paul (cf. Titus 1:5–9), took the lead in appointing church leaders. Rather, he stresses to these congregations the importance of their discernment of the character and qualifications of teachers (3:1–18). From Galatians 1, we discover something similar: apostolic authority was conditioned upon its submission to the truthfulness of the gospel it proclaimed. All human authority is subject to God and the gospel.

The number, functions, and interrelationships of the teachers and elders are also unclear. Are the elders all teachers? Are the teachers also elders? How are they distinguished? How closely do

29. Moo, *James*, PNTC, 102–3.
30. Schreiner, *New Testament Theology*, 742.

they reflect the positions in the Jewish synagogue? Unfortunately, James does not elaborate on such things. And since the letter is to multiple churches, it is impossible to know if he was speaking of singular or multiple persons per congregation.

Even more, the relationships among the church, the teachers, and the elders are fuzzy. The elders minister to the sick and pray over them, and are deemed the spiritual leaders of the churches. They are people of faith, the kind of people someone wants to pray for them. It is also possible from James 5:13–16 that they occasionally listen to the confessed sin of the sick. And the teachers obviously have authority or there would be no need for the warnings given to the church in James 3. Yet it is also significant that the church is to be careful concerning whom they trust as their teachers. Not all those who assert themselves as teachers should be recognized as such. Implicit throughout James 3 is that those who have the position of teacher, but who do not display fruit in keeping with the position, are not to be followed. So the teachers have authority, but not sweeping authority, as the congregations must evaluate their credibility.

Last Things

Eschatological themes in James are prominent. One clear example is the final judgment. As the Lawgiver and Judge, God is to be feared and obeyed (2:8–13; 4:11–12). He will bring about a final reversal, as we often find in the teachings of Jesus, in which the humble poor are ultimately exalted, and the arrogant rich are ultimately humiliated (1:9–11). The oppressed will be vindicated, and the oppressors will be oppressed by God himself (5:1–11).[31] Related to this final reversal are teachings about the coming of the Lord. Jesus' coming is viewed as future and near. His coming is "at hand" (5:8).

31. See Todd C. Penner, *The Epistle of James and Eschatology: Rereading an Ancient Christian Letter*, Journal for the Study of the New Testament, Supplement Series 121 (Sheffield: Sheffield Academic Press, 1996), 144–81.

Jesus' coming is also linked to his role as Judge: "Behold, the Judge is standing at the door" (5:9). This judgment is for believers and unbelievers, since judgment is promised to the oppressors (5:1–6), and brothers are warned not to grumble against one another (5:7–10), not to misuse oaths (5:12), and not to judge another brother (4:11–12) lest they be judged for it.

There are final states to be expected. Those in the covenant community who persevere in their faith in Christ will be blessed, receiving final salvation. This is a recurring theme. Those who respond to trials appropriately will become mature and perfect (1:2–8). The poor who humble themselves before the Lord now will receive final exaltation (1:9–11). Those who persevere and pass the test will receive the crown of life, promised to those who love God (1:12). Those who have been brought forth as a new creation are also firstfruits awaiting the display of the ultimate new creation (1:18). Those who receive the implanted word and follow it will be saved (1:21). Those who hear the word and do it will be blessed in their doing (1:25). Those who display their faith by loving the hurting, controlling their words, and being holy will be received and accepted by God (1:26–27). Indeed, the poor are chosen by God to be rich in faith and heirs of the kingdom (2:1–7). Genuine faith that results in following Christ and showing mercy to others will result in a merciful final justification (2:8–13, 14–26). God exalts, shows grace to, and draws near to those who submit to him and humble themselves before him (4:4–10). He forgives sin and includes the repentant in his kingdom (5:19–20).

The final state of the wicked is also taught. Unbelievers will receive final humiliation, passing away withered and scorched like the grass (1:9–11). Those following the path of temptation find that the offspring of desire is sin, and when sin develops, it brings death (1:13–15). Religious hypocrites will find that God rejects their religion as bogus (1:26–27). The merciless will find mercy withheld at the judgment (2:8–13). Those whose faith is not displayed in works of love will not be justified (2:14–26). The wicked have made God their enemy, receive opposition from God, and will face future destruction (4:1–12). They might wish that destruction were annihilation, but James adds that they will weep and howl because of their coming miseries. A related portrait is graphic: the wicked are fattened for the final slaughterhouse (5:1–6).[32] James states that whenever a believer restores a wanderer, he "will save his soul from death and will cover a multitude of sins" (5:20).

Jesus' coming, the judgment, the final reversal, the future punishment of the wicked, and the future blessedness of the saved are all linked together in James's thought. These truths should lead the people of God to faith, humility, mercy, hope, perseverance, and patience in the meantime.[33]

James also views salvation history in terms of the already and the not yet: the kingdom has already arrived, but has not yet been finally consummated. This shows itself in the church as the eschatological covenant community of believers, which is to be marked by unity, holiness, love, and truth, but still struggles with division, pride, hypocrisy, and slander. This also shows itself in the lives of believers, who are to be characterized by faith, humility, love, mercy to the poor, and self-control, but still struggle with pride, self-promotion, destructive speech, and inconsistency. For James, the kingdom, salvation, the church, and history are all eschatological in the sense of living in the tension of the already and the not yet.

James's eschatological approach to salvation history often reflects the imagery of exile and restoration and of wilderness and exodus. James writes to the twelve tribes in the Diaspora (1:1), which is probably best understood historically and theologically. These are churches composed of Jewish Christians living outside of Palestine, but they also constitute "the twelve tribes." Just as Jesus' appointment of twelve disciples symbolizes the reconstitution of Israel, so James's portrayal of the churches as the twelve

32. See Christopher W. Morgan and Robert A. Peterson, eds., *Hell under Fire: Modern Scholarship Reinvents Eternal Punishment* (Grand Rapids: Zondervan, 2004).
33. Mark A. Seifrid, "The Waiting Church and Its Duty: James 5:13–18," *Southern Baptist Journal of Theology* 4, no. 3 (Fall 2000): 32–39.

tribes draws attention to the church as the reconstituted and eschatological Israel. Further, James depicts the scattered people of God as oppressed under trials, which recalls Exodus 1–3, and as the poor, which resembles Isaiah's language of exile (26:6; 49:13; 51:21).

In this time of testing, the people of God are to pray to the Lord and display covenant faithfulness (1:2–8). He points to the future for the blessing of God that awaits all who persevere (1:12), and warns that they should not blame God for these tests, remembering that God is good and loves his covenant people (1:12–15). To be unfaithful to God and his covenant is to follow the way of sin, which leads to death (a covenant curse; cf. Deut. 30–31). The people should embrace the good God who brings them forth as a new creation, as firstfruits of the final restoration (1:15–18). They should receive the implanted word, which is able to save them (here is the language of exodus or deliverance). But this word must be genuinely heard (1:19–25; cf. Deut. 6:4–7)—not just with their ears, but in their lives. If it is, the people will display personal holiness that is reflective of God's character, will exercise self-control over their words, and will minister to the disadvantaged (cf. Lev. 11:44–45; Deut. 10:12–22). Otherwise, their worship will be defiled and unclean (1:26–27; 4:8; cf. Lev. 11). James urges respect for the poor, who are heirs of the kingdom and the promise, who bear the Lord's name, and who are therefore his people (2:1–7; cf. Deut. 10:12–22; 28:10). He also reminds people that obedience to God's commandments expresses love for others and demonstrates genuine faith (2:8–26; cf. Lev. 19; Deut. 5). For the well-being of the community, they must repent of pride, hypocrisy, and slander, which are likened to spiritual adultery, uncleanness, and judging (4:1–12).

The hope of the people is that the Lord hears their cries (5:1–6; cf. Ex. 1–3) and will come to judge the oppressors and deliver his people. Until the Lord's coming and the final restoration, the people of God must not grumble as the Israelites did in the wilderness (cf. Ex. 15–16), but be patient, promote community, and seek to restore the spiritual wanderers (5:7–20).

Thus, James emphasizes that salvation history is moving forward to realize God's intended purposes. Jesus will come in victory, judge the oppressors, and restore his people. In the meantime, the churches must respond appropriately to tests, remain faithful to the covenant, depend on him, strengthen (and not tear down) each other, not grumble, be patient, and restore the wanderers.

12

Theology at Work

HAVING EXAMINED the themes and theology of the epistle of James, the question emerges: how does James's theology function in the letter? James uses theology both to instruct and to exhort. In a nutshell, his exhortations are rooted in theology, and his theology is pastorally applied.

God at Work

James bases many of his exhortations on his doctrine of God. While he often does this implicitly, it is remarkable how often he does so explicitly. This tendency finds its roots in the Old Testament, as Christopher Wright observes:

> What shape, then, should Israel's response take? What was to be the substance and quality of their ethical behavior? Here again, the answer is thoroughly theological: nothing less than the reflection of the character of God. . . . That is why knowing God is such an important theme in the Old Testament. It means more than just what God has done (the stories), or knowing what God has said (the teachings). It means knowing the LORD in person, as a living character; knowing what his values, concerns and priorities are; knowing what brings him joy or makes him angry. And that in turn will mean living in the light of such knowledge.[1]

1. Christopher J. H. Wright, *Old Testament Ethics for the People of God* (Downers Grove, IL: InterVarsity Press, 2004), 36.

James's habit of grounding his exhortations in the doctrine of God also mirrors the teachings of Jesus, who routinely follows this pattern, as a few examples from the Sermon on the Mount reveal. Jesus commands us to love our enemies, so that we may bear a family resemblance to our Father in heaven, who sends the rain on the just and the unjust (Matt. 5:45). Jesus summarizes his hard claims, "Be perfect, as your heavenly Father is perfect" (Matt. 5:48). He teaches us not to worry, but to trust God, because God provides for us (Matt. 6:25–34).[2]

Two clarifications are in order. First, I do not mean that every time James teaches about God, he gives an exhortation. Sometimes he offers insights related to God or mentions that believers should be aware of the nature of God for other reasons. Second, I do not mean that every time James exhorts the believing community, he uses the doctrine of God as his foundation. James bases his practical advice on other doctrines as well, especially ecclesiology and eschatology. Further, sometimes his exhortations are based on a complex matrix of teachings, especially the foundation of love for one another. This complexity is explained by Luke Johnson:

> James's ethical teaching, in fact, is closely connected to his theology and finds its basis in his theological perceptions. Among the attempts to characterize the theological framework more completely are those that focus on its grounding in the cult, in the word of God, in wisdom, or even in Christology. All of these investigations agree that James's moral discourse is deeply embedded in the theological convictions of Judaism and the nascent Christian community.[3]

2. Concerning the relationship between Jesus' doctrine of God and his eschatology and his view of the kingdom, see G. E. Ladd, *The Presence of the Future: The Eschatology of Biblical Realism* (Grand Rapids: Eerdmans, 1974), 171.

3. Luke Timothy Johnson, *The Letter of James*, The Anchor Bible (New York: Doubleday, 1995), 159–60. Johnson refers to C. E. B. Cranfield, "The Message of James," *Southwestern Journal of Theology* 18 (1965): 182–93, 338–45; Sophie Laws, "The Doctrinal Basis for the Ethics of James," *Studia Evangelica* 7 (1982): 299–305; James B. Adamson, *James: The Man and His Message* (Grand Rapids: Eerdmans, 1989), 259–471; R. B. Ward, "The Communal Concern of the Epistle of James," (PhD diss., Harvard University, 1966).

Those who have highlighted James's overall tendency to base his practical advice on his doctrine of God include John Mahony, H. Frankemölle, Douglas Moo, and Alec Motyer.[4] Motyer sees James 1:26–27 as central:

> There is a natural sequence about it: (i) the new birth (18–19a); (ii) the growth of the new life (19b–25); and (iii) the characteristics that the new life displays (26–27). This sequence is bound together by the fact that the same three features are central to the acts of God the Father (18) and the acts of his new-born children (26–27): he first reached out to us through the life-giving word he spoke, that is, "the word of truth" (18), and we ... should be marked by a bridled tongue (26). Behind his spoken word lay that act of his will whereby he determined what he would do for us (18), depraved in nature and death-bound though we were (14–15). In a word, our Father cares about the needy, and so should we (27a). But his life-giving work for us had a purpose, "the first fruits" (18), namely that we be specially his and notably holy. Therefore we ought to bear the mark of personal holiness unstained from the world (27b).
>
> The three Christian characteristics of verses 26–27 are thus not an arbitrary choice. They say to us "Like Father, like child."

These scholars point us in the right direction. James's theology is at work as he grounds many of his exhortations on his doctrine of God. We turn now to see how he does so.

James 1:5–8

Ben Witherington notices the tendency in James 1:1–18 to base exhortations on the doctrine of God. He asserts: "It is a mistake to see the material in this discourse as just parenesis or hortatory in character. It would be better to call it theological ethics, as it is grounded

---

4. John W. Mahony, "The Origin of Jacobean Thought" (PhD diss., Mid-America Baptist Theological Seminary, 1982), 79–84; H. Frankemölle, "Das semantische Netz des Jakobusbriefes: Zur Einheit eines unstritten Briefes," *Biblische Zeitschrift* 34 (1990): 190–93; Douglas J. Moo, *The Letter of James*, Pillar New Testament Commentary (Grand Rapids: Eerdmans, 2000), 28; J. A. Motyer, *The Message of James*, Bible Speaks Today (Downers Grove, IL: InterVarsity Press, 1985), 73–74.

in a certain view of God and divine activity, as this paragraph makes so apparent. God is the one who sends wisdom, gives every good gift (including perseverance) and is the model of rectitude."[5]

James 1:2–8 encourages those facing trials to consider it all joy and to let perseverance finish its work, and then he urges those who lack wisdom to ask God for it. On what basis should they do so? The nature of God. James here assumes the Old Testament idea that God is the source of wisdom (Prov. 2:6, "The Lord gives wisdom"), echoes Jesus' teaching in Matthew 7:7, and stresses that God gives wisdom generously to all without finding fault. We ask God for wisdom in the midst of trials because he generously gives wisdom to those who ask him for it. Even more, our asking should coincide with the way God gives—with single-mindedness, not double-mindedness.[6] God responds to our prayers when they reflect our spiritual integrity, a basic characteristic of which God himself is our example. Ralph Martin observes: "Hence it is appropriate to stress the character of God. There are three reasons supplied to encourage the approach in prayer. God is good to all who call on him; he gives with an open hand and without reservation; and his giving is not intended to demean the recipient with feelings that God is reproachful or reluctant to give what is for our good" (cf. Luke 11:5–8).[7]

James 1:12–18

Wall asserts that in 1:12–18 James "intends to form an understanding of God that prevents spiritual failure."[8] Wall adds:

5. Ben Witherington III, *Letters and Homilies for Jewish Christians: A Socio-Rhetorical Commentary on Hebrews, James and Jude* (Downers Grove, IL: InterVarsity Press, 2007), 420.

6. Moo, *James*, PNTC, 60. John Calvin comments on James 1:8: "This sentence may be read by itself, as he speaks generally of hypocrites. It seems, however, to me to be rather the conclusion of the preceding doctrine; and thus there is an implied contrast between the simplicity or liberality of God, mentioned before, and the double-mindedness of man; for as God gives to us with a stretched-out hand, so it behooves us in our turn to open the bosom of our heart." John Calvin, *Commentaries on the Catholic Epistles*, trans. John Owen, Calvin's Commentaries (repr., Grand Rapids: Baker, 1979), 284.

7. Ralph P. Martin, *James*, Word Biblical Commentary (Waco, TX: Word, 1988), 21.

8. Robert W. Wall, *Community of the Wise: The Letter of James*, New Testament in Context (Valley Forge, PA: Trinity Press International, 1997), 60.

James, which is a book of biblical wisdom, understands that theology is always cashed out in human actions, especially when faith in God is tested by hardship. The images of an empowering God in James are deliberately cast to form a theology that supplies a viable resource for a powerless people. These are the issues of theodicy. James raises the pastoral issues tied to this difficult problem: who is the God who stands with us in our trials and can we trust God to help us in the time of our need?[9]

James warns us not to blame God for our temptations. Instead of looking to God as the source, we should look within—at our own evil desires.

What is his basis for this exhortation? Again, it is the nature of God. "For God cannot be tempted with evil, and he himself tempts no one" (1:13). God is holy and never the source of temptations. God is not our foe, but our covenant Lord. He is for us, not against us. Indeed, God is the source of "every good gift and every perfect gift" (1:17). He is "the Father of lights with whom there is no variation" (1:17). As Peter Davids comments, "God neither changes nor is changed."[10] He has no dark side, but is unchangingly good—giving new life, not spiritual death. Thus, a right understanding of God leads the believing community to trust and turn to him for aid in the midst of trials and temptations.[11]

James 1:26-27

Considering James 1:19–27, Witherington comments, "Our discourse is about a God who is impartial, faithful, righteous, just, merciful—and who requires of his followers the same sort of behavior."[12] The last part of this discourse is particularly instructive. The religion that God accepts as pure and undefiled involves looking after orphans and widows in their distress and refraining from being polluted by the world (1:27).

9. Ibid., 60.
10. Peter H. Davids, *The Epistle of James*, New International Greek Testament Commentary (Grand Rapids: Eerdmans, 1982), 88.
11. Wall, *Community of the Wise*, 60–61.
12. Witherington, *Letters and Homilies for Jewish Christians*, 436.

On what basis does James commend this behavior? The nature and standards of God. Here the nature of God is not explicitly described, but rather is presupposed. James's readers knew that God is a "father of the fatherless and protector of widows" (Ps. 68:5). Just as God defends and cares for the widows and the fatherless, so must his people. The needy must not be subjected to abuse, but must be protected. Wall adds:

> What a person thinks and knows about God and self determines the decisions made during trials. . . . Yet for James, every deception, as well as every test, is theological in nature (cf. 1:16, 22). In this case, the theological crisis is theodicy: the fool miscalculates God's sense of justice. . . . The fool supposes than an offering of pious slogans rather than of merciful work satisfies God, whose primary concern is that justice is executed for the widow and orphan in distress. . . .
>
> Of course, passing the test has everything to do with the way one "thinks" (1:2) and what one knows (1:3): an "ethics of doing" is grounded in an "ethics of seeing." Therefore, if one is mistaken about God's role in human suffering (1:13–15), one's performance of religious sentiment is "worthless" to God.[13]

Daniel Doriani captures the idea marvelously: "Kindness to the needy is God-like. *We* sustain aliens, widows, and orphans because *he* sustains aliens, widows, and orphans (Ps. 146:9)."[14]

Further, James points to our need for holiness as he urges Christians to be "unstained from the world" (1:27). God's own holiness calls us, his covenant people, to holiness, as Leviticus 19:2 reminds us: "You shall be holy, for I the LORD your God am holy" (cf. 1 Peter 1:15–16).

James 2:1–7

James 2:1–7 urges believers not to show favoritism toward the rich and against the poor. James offers an example of a church

---

13. Wall, *Community of the Wise*, 99.
14. Daniel M. Doriani, *James*, Reformed Expository Commentary (Phillipsburg, NJ: P&R Publishing, 2007), 59 (emphasis in original).

community giving the red-carpet treatment to the rich but disregarding the poor. While there are various reasons put forward for not showing partiality, a primary one is that God chose the poor to be rich in faith and inherit the kingdom. God chose the poor, so why should we neglect or reject them?

Wall argues that James's views on God and last things serve as the foundation for this exhortation: "God stands on the side of those the powerful of this world exploit and the people of God ignore: the very act of choosing the poor conjugates the impartial character of God's coming reign. . . . The act of divine election presumes the responsibility of those elected: the moral obligation of the faith community is to herald this coming age by elevating their status in the present age."[15]

James 2:8-13

James 2:8–13 continues James's rebuke of those who show favoritism and points out that such behavior is inconsistent with Leviticus 19:18 and Jesus' teaching about loving others. He also shows that it breaks God's law. He points to the unity of the law and adds, "So speak and so act as those who are to be judged under the law of liberty" (2:12).

Why? Because God is the Lawgiver and the Judge. The law reflects the will of the Lawgiver, so to violate it is to be unfaithful to God and his covenant. God's law is serious, and his judgment will be without mercy to those who show no mercy. Because of this, believers are to obey his law.

In addition, because God is merciful, his people should show mercy. Moo explains: "God, the NT suggests, delights especially to shower his grace on those whom the world has discarded and on those most keenly aware of their own inadequacy. James calls on the church to embody a similar ethic of special concern for the poor and the helpless."[16]

15. Wall, *Community of the Wise*, 114–15.
16. Moo, *James*, PNTC, 108. Cf. Andrew Chester and Ralph P. Martin, *The Theology of the Letters of James, Peter, and Jude*, New Testament Theology (New York: Cambridge University Press, 1996), 33–34.

James 4:1–10

James 4:1–10 puts forward commands almost in staccato form, with verses 7–10 containing a series of stock exhortations. Throughout are truths about God. God is jealous (4:4), opposes the proud, gives grace to the humble (4:6), and is personal (4:8, "Draw near to God, and he will draw near to you"). The point is clear: because of God's nature and ways, we should respond to him appropriately. God requires our single-minded devotion (cf. 1:8). He resists the proud and gives grace to the humble, so we should humble ourselves before the Lord and receive his exaltation. God is jealous, so we must not be spiritual adulterers with the world. God is holy, so we must come to him seriously grieved over our sin, seeking repentance and genuinely desiring him.

James 4:11–12

James 4:11–12 again deals with God as the only Lawgiver and Judge. James commands believers not to slander one another, which is in essence speaking against the law, breaking it, and judging it. Such speech is unacceptable because "there is only one lawgiver and judge, he who is able to save and to destroy" (4:12). Moo states it well: slandering one another is wrong because it "involves an infringement of the unique right of God himself."[17] Johnson observes: "As always in James, the theological statement serves as warrant for moral exhortation: it is because God alone has power of life and death that God alone has the right to reveal the law and judge by the law. Any human seizure of that right—especially in secret—is revealed as pitiful pretension."[18] James's warning seems odd in our era where doctors are sometimes charged with "playing God"; criticizing others is sinful partly because it is "playing God," proudly claiming for ourselves his unique prerogative.

17. Moo, *James*, PNTC, 199.
18. Johnson, *The Letter of James*, 307.

James 4:13-17

James 4:13-17 warns believers to be careful not to be presumptuous in their plans or arrogant in their claims. Why? James supplies multiple reasons. First, we do not know the future, so how can we guarantee our plans? Second, our lives are short, and we cannot even control how long we live. But the foundational reason is that the Lord is sovereign, and we are not. It is he who guides history according to his will. We recognize his sovereign lordship, reject our pride, and submit our plans to his will. Because no part of life is outside the rule of God, all of our plans should be conditioned by his will and should recognize both human finitude and divine sovereignty.[19]

James 5:1-11

James 5:1-11 thunders a warning of the divine judgment coming upon exploitive landowners, who should weep and wail because of the severe and impending judgment. James then encourages God's people to be patient and stand firm.

On what basis does James make this appeal? On the nature of God, who hears the cries of the oppressed and is the Lord of hosts, the all-knowing warrior who avenges his people. Linking God's triumph over evil with the establishment of his reign, Wall observes:

> The cries of the fieldhands have reached the ears of God (cf. Isa. 5:9). God's interest in their situation is understood by the Hebrew title given, "the Lord Sabaoth." Its full meaning is discerned only in conversation with the biblical prophets (esp. Isaiah, Jeremiah, and Zechariah) who speak of the Lord as a warrior God, leading to victory "armies" of faithful Jews over Israel's (=God's) enemies. More importantly, the Lord's coming to do battle against evil marks the close of the present age during which time the rich continue to oppress the poor, often with impunity.[20]

19. Davids, *James*, 173.
20. Wall, *Community of the Wise*, 231-32.

Because God is a warrior, those who oppress his people had better prepare for their just judgment, and his people need to persevere in the midst of these trials.

James continues, stressing the need to be patient and stand firm because the Lord's coming is near. This should not lead us to presumption, but to carefulness. We must not grumble against one another, because we too will be judged. Indeed the Judge is nearby, standing at the threshold! In sum, the nature of God and his eschatological victory and judgment incites us to patience, standing firm, and love for one another, with no room for grumbling.

James then points to the prophets and Job as examples of those blessed through persevering. James wants his readers to persevere as those Old Testament heroes did. He then tells them why: "The Lord is compassionate and merciful" (5:11). James's teaching recalls Exodus 34:6–7, where the Lord proclaimed himself as "the LORD, a God merciful and gracious, slow to anger, and abounding in steadfast love and faithfulness, keeping steadfast love for thousands, forgiving iniquity and transgression and sin, but who will by no means clear the guilty" (cf. Ps. 103:8). The motivation for their perseverance and hope is clear, says Doriani: "God is not vicious; he does not love watching people suffer. Rather he is compassionate."[21] Doriani develops the point further: "This passage offers us many reasons to persevere in the faith. It comforts us in several ways. First, it shows us the Lord. He is near. He is the Judge and comes to set all things straight. Second, it reminds us of Job and the prophets, who persevered to the end in great adversity. Yet above all, James takes us to the fatherly heart of God. He abounds in love and he is sovereign still."[22]

James 5:13–20

James concludes his letter with specific appeals. Each appeal is tied to the nature of the Christian community, but also to the

21. Doriani, James, 183.
22. Ibid., 184.

nature and work of God—some directly and others somewhat indirectly. God heals, so we are to pray for the sick (5:15). God answers prayer, as Elijah discovered, so we should pray for each other in faith (5:15). God forgives sin, so we are to confess our sins (5:16). This pattern extends to James's last exhortation. God forgives and is a God of truth, so we must seek to restore those wandering from the truth (5:19–20).

Synthesis: Theology at Work

James writes, not to set forth a theological system, but to cultivate wisdom for consistency in the communities to which he is writing. However, his robust theology, and especially his doctrine of God, often serves as the basis of his appeals to the churches.

Roots in the Old Testament

The relationship between theology and ethical exhortation seen in James is found throughout the Old Testament, particularly in several texts to which James alludes. For example, it is well recognized that James makes use of Leviticus 19.[23] What is rarely noticed, however, is that this passage follows the same approach to God-centered ethics as James. Leviticus 19:2 states, "Be holy, for I the LORD your God am holy." In what ways was Israel supposed to be holy? Commenting on Leviticus 19 (not having James in mind), Wright observes:

> We are inclined to think of "holiness" as a matter of personal piety or, in Old Testament terms, of ritual cleanness, proper sacrifices, clean and unclean foods, and the like. Certainly, the rest of Leviticus 19 includes some of these dimensions of Israel's religious life. But the bulk of the chapter shows us that the kind of holiness that reflects God's own holiness is thoroughly practical. It includes generosity to the poor at harvest time, justice for

23. Luke Timothy Johnson, "The Use of Leviticus 19 in the Letter of James," *Journal of Biblical Literature* 101, no. 3 (1982): 391–402.

workers, integrity in judicial processes, considerate behavior to other people (especially the disabled), equality before the law for immigrants, honest trading and other very "earthy" social matters. And all throughout the chapters runs the refrain "I am the LORD," as if to say, "Your quality of life must reflect the very heart of my character. This is what I require of you because this is what reflects me."[24]

Many other Old Testament texts to which James alludes, besides Leviticus 19, ground commands in the doctrine of God. James 1:5–8, like Proverbs 2:6, urges people to seek wisdom from God because he is its source and gives it generously. James 1:13–18, like Genesis 1, teaches that the good God blesses with good gifts; he is not the source of evil. James 1:26–27, like Psalm 68:5, Exodus 22:22, and Isaiah 1:10–17, points to God's concern for, and the necessity of Israel's concern for, the widow and the orphan. James 2:1–13 and texts like Leviticus 19 urge the loving treatment of others, especially the poor and marginalized, because of the nature of God. James 4, like Exodus 20:5 and Deuteronomy 34:14, points to the need for covenant fidelity because God is jealous. James 4:6, following Proverbs 3:34, urges believers to be humble because God opposes the proud and gives grace to the humble. James 4:11–12 follows Leviticus 19 in warning against slander because of the unity of the law and the authority of the Lawgiver. James 5:1–11 again reflects Leviticus 19 as it warns against withholding wages from day laborers because of God's concern for the oppressed. James 5:11 quotes Exodus 34:6 to promote perseverance in the midst of adversity by reminding us of the covenant faithfulness of God.

Roots in Jesus' Teachings

Furthermore, James follows the example of Jesus in this approach. Like Jesus, James exhorts his hearers to adopt particular attitudes and behaviors because of the nature of God.

---

24. Wright, *Old Testament Ethics for the People of God*, 39.

James 1:5–8, like Jesus in Matthew 7:7–11, urges people to ask in faith because of the goodness of God. Similarly, James 1:15–18 speaks of God being good and the giver of good gifts to his children. James 2:1–7 follows Matthew 5:3 and Luke 6:20 in linking the poor to the kingdom, and follows Luke 12:21 in stressing the need to be rich toward God. James 2:8–13 resembles Matthew 5:17–20 and 22:34–40 in emphasizing love and the unity and abiding value of the law, as well as the consequent seriousness of a seemingly small infraction. James 2:8–13 and 4:11–12 reflect Jesus' emphasis in Matthew 5:7; 7:1–12; 18:21–35 that how a person judges others affects the strictness with which God judges him. The idea is to show mercy because God shows mercy to the merciful. James 4:1–10 recalls Matthew 5:4–8 and 7:7–8, when it commends mourning and purity of heart, as well as praying in faith. Similarly, James 4:1–10 brings to mind Matthew 23:12 and Luke 14:11, teaching that one should be humble and not exalt oneself because of the paradox that God exalts the humble. James 4:13–16, like Matthew 6:34, reminds us of our need to trust God due to his providence.

It is unclear whether James intentionally follows the example of God-based exhortations in Leviticus 19, other Old Testament texts, and the teachings of Jesus. I suspect that James reflects their pattern more intuitively.

One thing is certain: James advances a robust view of God that shapes not only our theology but also our very lives. Because of who God is, in faith we ask him for wisdom, live consistently, fight temptation, control our speech, take care of the marginalized, reject favoritism, meet the needs of the poor, humble ourselves, worship with genuineness, do not slander, make plans in submission to his sovereignty, live in patience and hope, and become people of prayer and forgiveness.

Eschatology at Work

James not only roots many of his exhortations in the doctrine of God, but also grounds many of them in eschatology. That

James's ethical teaching is eschatologically based is manifest in several passages.

James 1 encourages us to "count it all joy" when trials come, so that we "may be perfect and complete" (1:2–4). James urges us to boast in our future exaltation and the final punishment of wicked oppressors (1:9–11). James also points to the eschatological blessedness of persevering under trial, for we will receive the crown of life (1:12). He warns that yielding to temptation will result in death (1:13–15), and stresses that God's goodness leads to our new creation as firstfruits of a future harvest, which is probably to be understood as the eschatological new creation (1:16–18). James urges us to use words carefully and to receive the implanted word, because it is able to save our souls (1:19–21). He also commands us not only to hear the word, but also to do it, because we will be blessed in our doing (1:22–25).

James 2 requires us to treat the poor with love and respect, in part because God has chosen them to be heirs of the kingdom (2:1–7). We must love and show mercy because we will face the final judgment, which will be linked to whether we display mercy (2:8–13). He then demands that our faith be consistent, manifesting itself in works of love for the poor. Such faith is real and will be accepted by God in the end; bogus faith will be rejected (2:14–26).

James 3 warns potential teachers that they will face a stricter judgment (3:1). It also teaches that genuine wisdom shows itself through various works and that "a harvest of righteousness is sown in peace by those who make peace" (3:18). Because of this, we should select our words and our church leaders carefully.

James 4 demands our submission and humility before God because God resists the proud and gives grace to the humble, whom he will exalt (4:1–10). James 4:11–12 warns us not to slander others, because we will stand before the Lawgiver and Judge, who is able to save and to destroy. James 4:13–17 instructs us to submit ourselves to God's providential control, in part, because our lives are short.

James's use of eschatology as a basis for exhortations becomes most forceful in chapter 5. The oppressive rich are to weep over, and the righteous poor are to find comfort in, the future punishment and suffering of the wicked (5:1–6). As Christ's people, we are to be patient and to establish our hearts because "the coming of the Lord is at hand" (5:7–8). We are also forbidden to grumble against one another, because the Judge is nearby (5:9). Wall notes:

> What was implicit to this point in James is now made dramatically evident and concrete: the way of wisdom must be followed because the coming of the Lord is "at hand" and the Judge is "standing at the doors." The author's confidence in the coming triumph of the Lord provides the readership with its most compelling reason to be "quick to hear, slow to speak, slow to anger"; indeed to refuse this advice is to miss out on anticipated blessing and face God's judgment instead. The imminency of the Lord's *parousia* only makes more urgent and necessary the community's wise response to spiritual testing. . . . The importance of eschatology for ethics is well established: how we view the future determines in part what we do in the present.[25]

James 5:10–11 also encourages us to be patient, because only those who remain steadfast will be blessed. Wall again is helpful:

> To endure to the end is to be "blessed"—yet another element of the eschatological matrix introduced in James 1:12 and repeated here to conclude the book. According to 1:12, the patient response to suffering is viewed as an act of loving devotion to God. In this setting, however, the emphasis is on the Lord's response to the faithful congregation rather than the reverse: the Lord comes with compassion and mercy to those who have passed their spiritual tests. The whole point nicely defines the covenantal reciprocity of salvation's history: the promise of salvation, offered and fulfilled by a "compassionate and merciful" God, is realized

25. Wall, *Community of the Wise*, 249–50.

in that eschatological community that responds in love toward God. . . . The dividend of faithfulness to God in the crucible of life's circumstances, when a "compassionate and merciful" Lord seems at times utterly absent, is the full and concrete demonstration and vindication of divine love at the *parousia*.[26]

Even the reason for the prohibition of oaths is "so that you may not fall under condemnation" (5:12). Praying in faith "will save the one who is sick, and the Lord will raise him up" (5:15). And if he has committed sins, "he will be forgiven" (5:15). James ends with an appeal to eschatological truths: we should seek to bring the wanderer back because that "will save his soul from death and will cover a multitude of sins" (5:19–20).

For James, eschatology is not merely a topic to be studied. James wants the realities of eschatological testing, final judgment, final salvation, and final blessedness to drive us to joy, perseverance, controlled speech, obedience, holiness, support for the disadvantaged, respect for the poor, mercy for the destitute, careful selection of church leaders, submission, humility, appropriate planning, comfort, patience, stability, faith, prayer, and the restoration of wanderers. Eschatology is at work, compelling us to lives of covenant faithfulness.

The Church at Work

James's ethical teaching is also rooted in his ecclesiology. This is especially evident in the last half of the epistle. James warns against certain people becoming teachers, in part because of the damage that sinful speech causes in churches (3:1–12). He lists character traits of genuine wisdom, so that believers will know how to identify mature and worthy leaders. In doing this, James lists traits that we should embody, traits that edify and bring peace to churches, such as meekness, purity, gentleness, reasonableness, mercy, goodness, impartiality, sincerity, humility, and peace (3:13–18). He also warns us against pride, jealousy, selfish

26. Ibid., 258.

ambition, and divisiveness, which damage covenant communities (3:13–18).

James also cautions us about covetousness, hate, pride, slander, and judgmental attitudes, because such things hurt churches (4:1–12). He teaches us to be humble before the Lord, which strengthens community relationships (4:1–12).

In chapter 5, James bases several exhortations on his view of the church. Because the church is an eschatological community, we must be patient until the consummation comes (5:1–11). In the meantime, we live in a world of sickness and sin. These realities of the present age directly affect the church, so we pray over the sick (5:13–15), confess sin to one another (5:16), and seek to restore one another (5:19–20).

For James, a sound view of the church is crucial because it leads to the careful selection of teachers, controlled speech, the promotion of unity, the development of humility, the rejection of slander, and a community of prayer, confession, restoration, and love. Indeed, personal ethics are closely linked to social ethics,[27] or better, church ethics.

Thus, James roots his ethical instruction in the doctrines of God, last things, and the church. James's exhortations are theologically rooted, and his theology is pastorally applied. For James, theology is at work, fostering wisdom for consistency in the churches.

---

27. Mariam Kamell, "The Economics of Humility: The Rich and the Humble in James," in *Economic Dimensions of Early Christianity*, ed. Bruce Longenecker and Kelly Leibengood (Grand Rapids: Eerdmans, 2009), 157–75.

13

James for the Twenty-first–Century Church

"JAMES'S THEOLOGICAL and literary genius and uniqueness lie in his ability to blend theology into the immediate application. He does not first have to lay down theological principles from which he draws applications."[1] Because of this, as we have studied James's theology, we have also encountered many specific applications. Indeed, as I have been writing this book, I have been regularly thinking of areas in my own life that need to be addressed. Who among us does not need to be more consistent, to seek wisdom more seriously, to respond with more faith to suffering, to care more for the disadvantaged, or to be more submissive to God's word? Those matters are of great importance to all of us. Here, however, I want to draw attention to four broader aspects of James's message that are particularly timely for today's church.

The first of these, related to the quote above, is that James views truth holistically. His holistic approach can serve as a helpful corrective to our contemporary false dichotomies or polarizations. Many evangelicals today have a tendency to separate such things as love for God and love for others, faith and works, evangelism and social ministry, and theology and practice. In contrast, James sees that these things function together. He insists that a life

1. David P. Scaer, *James: The Apostle of Faith: A Primary Christological Epistle for the Persecuted Church* (St. Louis: Concordia, 1994), 60.

poured out in service of God is a life of ministering God's love to others. Those with faith in Christ follow Christ. A heart that cares for people's salvation inevitably seeks their overall good, spiritually and physically. The word of God requires careful thinking and consistent implementation. Such a holistic approach pervades James and is worthy of our rediscovery.

From James we also learn that Christianity brings a reversal of values. Reflective of Jesus' Sermon on the Mount, James notes this reversal in a number of areas. Instead of seeking positions to gain power, church leaders are granted authority to serve others. Instead of fighting to promote our agenda, we are to seek what is good for the church. Rather than currying the favor of influential people in society, we minister to the marginalized. Rather than assuming our own power to accomplish our plans, we recognize our creaturely dependence on God's sovereignty. Churches and church leaders have a tendency to reflect the society around them, but James presses us to think and act differently. After all, we are a part of a new society, the community of Jesus.

Third, while those of us from the Reformed tradition have rightly emphasized the importance of the covenant for theology, I fear that we do not sufficiently stress the importance of covenant faithfulness. The covenant *is* a helpful paradigm for understanding the biblical theology, *but it also makes demands upon us*. James continually presses the importance of our faithfulness to God. Yes, God's grace has initiated, has brought about, sustains, and ultimately preserves our salvation. But this leads us to assurance only if it is linked to our faith, obedience, and love. Salvation is all of grace, but that grace is never divorced from our fruit or perseverance.

Finally, as I have wrestled with the message of James for several years now, one truth keeps emerging, one that might be the most needed by the church today: James's view of the church itself. A lot of ink is being spilled regarding the purpose, style, and functions of the church, and these are important matters. But more foundational is what the church actually *is*, and James helps us with this. Although the church is not yet all it is intended to be, and is still riddled with hypocrisy, inconsistency, pride, and division, it is an eschatological covenant community that exists in the already and the not yet and thus displays (even if imperfectly) the arrival of the kingdom through its relationships to God, among its members, and to society. Longing for the final arrival of the kingdom, the people of Jesus pursue and foster wholeness. The church is an eschatological, covenantal, worshipping community of believers, created and shaped by the word, where the truth is taught, love for one another is genuine, mercy to the poor is shown, mutuality and accountability are evident, and wanderers are restored. It is God's new creation, exemplifying the arrival of the kingdom as the firstfruits of the way things should and will be (1:18). As the church displays the way of the kingdom, it pleases God as acceptable and pure (1:26–27), and it shines as a light to the world, as a blessing to the nations. Tim Keller captures the importance of this for today's church:

> Jesus calls Christians to be "witnesses," to evangelize others, but also to be deeply concerned for the poor. He calls his disciples *both* to "gospel-messaging" (urging everyone to believe the gospel) *and* to "gospel-neighboring" (sacrificially meeting the needs of those around them, whether they believe or not!). The two absolutely go together. (1) They go together theologically. The resurrection shows us that God not only created both body and spirit but will also *redeem* both body and spirit. The salvation Jesus will eventually bring in its fullness will include liberation from *all* the effects of sin—not only spiritual but physical and material as well. Jesus came both preaching the Word and healing and feeding. (2) They go together practically. We must be ever wary of collapsing evangelism into deed ministry as the social gospel did, but loving deeds are an irreplaceable witness to the power and nature of God's grace, an irreplaceable testimony to the truth of the gospel.[2]

Even James's call for wisdom for consistency in the communities is not an end in itself. It is intended to strengthen Christ's church, enhance our witness, and glorify God.

2. Tim Keller, "The Gospel and the Poor," *Themelios* 33, no. 3 (December 2008): 18 (emphasis in original).

Questions for Study and Reflection

Chapter 1—James in Context

1. Before reading this chapter, what did you know about the man James?

2. How does what you learned about the man James from reading this chapter help you understand his letter?

3. What difference does it make to read James as a letter written to Jewish Christians?

4. What are some characteristics of the churches to which James writes? How does knowing these characteristics help you understand his purpose in writing?

5. Once we see that James was a minister writing to help churches, how do we understand the letter better?

Chapter 2—Influences on James's Thought

1. What are the major influences on James's thought?

2. In what ways does James reflect Old Testament teachings?

3. James often reflects the teachings of Jesus. Reread James. How many examples did you find?

191

4. How does identifying such influences on James's thought help you understand his message?

Chapter 3—James's Pastoral Burden: Wisdom for Consistency in the Community

1. What does the author mean by James's pastoral burden?

2. List some places where this pastoral burden comes through.

3. Explain the author's idea of wisdom for consistency in the community.

4. Why is taking this community aspect into account important for understanding James? Cite a few examples.

Chapter 4—Wisdom

1. Summarize the four principles that James teaches concerning wisdom. How do these compare with how our contemporary culture thinks about wisdom?

2. In what ways does James reflect the Old Testament in his teachings concerning wisdom?

3. Describe the way James relates wisdom to faith.

4. Why is it so important that pastors, teachers, and church leaders are wise?

Chapter 5—Consistency

1. List as many of the principles related to consistency as you can.

2. How does James's teaching on consistency reflect Jesus' teaching on hypocrisy?

3. Explain James's idea of double-mindedness. Why is it important?

4. What damage does inconsistency cause in the church? What damage does it cause to the church's witness?

Chapter 6—Suffering

1. What types of suffering were faced by the churches to which James writes?

2. What are some of James's key teachings related to suffering? How do these truths help the churches?

3. Name some proper responses to suffering—from the sufferer's standpoint.

4. What are some proper responses to suffering—from the ministering church's standpoint? How can you and your church improve in this area?

Chapter 7—The Poor

1. List the various meanings of "the poor" in Scripture.

2. What are some of James's key teachings related to the poor?

3. Which of those teachings do you find the hardest to follow? Why?

4. How is your church ministering to the poor?

5. How can you and your church grow in this area?

Chapter 8—Words

1. What are some of James's key teachings related to words?

2. How does recognizing that James writes to the church help you understand his famous instruction related to the tongue?

3. Our words reflect our consistency or our inconsistency. Explain.

4. What is the relationship between our words and wisdom?

Chapter 9—God's Word and Law

1. What terms does James use to depict God's word and law?

2. What truths about God's word and law does James teach?

3. Summarize what James means by word and law.

4. What does James mean when he asserts that the law is a unity? Why does he say this?

5. James teaches that the law reflects the will of the Lawgiver. How can this help us understand and apply God's law to our lives?

Chapter 10—James and Paul

1. Were you previously troubled by James's and Paul's seemingly conflicting teachings on justification?

2. What were your thoughts on this issue prior to reading this chapter?

3. What questions should be asked, and in what order? Why does this matter here?

4. How are James's and Paul's doctrines of salvation similar?

5. How do their emphases differ? Why do we need both in today's church?

Chapter 11—A Sketch of James's Theology

1. Did you know how much James teaches about God prior to reading this chapter?

2. Reread James to answer the question: what truths does James teach about God?

3. What does James teach about Christ?

4. Summarize James's teaching on sin. How is this important for today's church?

5. What does James teach about the church? How is it important today?

6. How does James's teaching about last things impact churches today?

Chapter 12—Theology at Work

1. Would you describe James's theology as abstract or pastoral? Why?

2. How does James's message about God shape his exhortations?

3. How does James's instruction concerning the church affect his practical advice?

4. How does James apply his teachings on last things to the lives of his readers? How can this help us today?

Chapter 13—James for the Twenty-first-Century Church

1. In what areas has James's message challenged your life?

2. How is it helpful to view truth holistically? What happens when we do not?

3. How does James display a reversal of values? How does this help us look at life today?

4. What aspects of James's teaching on the church are most needed in your church? In other churches you know?

5. How is the effectiveness of the church's mission linked to the church's embodiment of Jesus' values?

Select Resources on James's Theology

Adamson, James B. *The Epistle of James.* New International Commentary on the New Testament. Grand Rapids: Eerdmans, 1976.

_____. *James: The Man and His Message.* Grand Rapids: Eerdmans, 1989.

Baker, William R. "Christology in the Epistle of James." *Evangelical Quarterly* 74, no. 1 (2002): 47–57.

_____. *Personal Speech-Ethics in the Epistle of James.* Tübingen: Mohr, 1995.

_____. "Searching for the Holy Spirit in James: Is Wisdom Equivalent?" *Tyndale Bulletin* 50, no. 2 (November 2008): 293–320.

_____. "Who's Your Daddy? Gendered Birth Images in the Soteriology of the Epistle of James (1:14–15, 18, 21)." *Evangelical Quarterly* 79, no. 3 (2007): 195–207.

Bauckham, Richard. *James: Wisdom of James, Disciple of Jesus the Sage.* London: Routledge, 1999.

Blomberg, Craig L., and Mariam J. Kamell. *James.* Zondervan Exegetical Commentary on the New Testament. Grand Rapids: Zondervan, 2008.

Carson, D. A. "James." In *Commentary on the New Testament Use of the Old Testament*, edited by D. A. Carson and G. K. Beale, 997–1013. Grand Rapids: Baker, 2007.

Chester, Andrew, and Ralph P. Martin. *The Theology of the Letters of James, Peter, and Jude*. New Testament Theology. Cambridge: Cambridge University Press, 1994.

Cheung, Luke L. *The Genre, Composition, and Hermeneutics of James*. Waynesboro, GA: Paternoster, 2003.

Davids, Peter H. "James and Jesus." In *Gospel Perspectives, Volume 5: The Jesus Tradition Outside the Gospels*, edited by David Wenham, 63–84. Sheffield: JSOT, 1985.

_____. *The Epistle of James*. New International Greek New Testament Commentary. Grand Rapids: Eerdmans, 1982.

Dockery, David S. "True Piety in James: Ethical Admonitions and Theological Implications." *Criswell Theological Review* 1, no. 1 (Fall 1986): 51–70.

Doriani, Daniel M. *James*. Reformed Expository Commentary. Phillipsburg, NJ: P&R Publishing, 2007.

Fung, Ronald Y. K. "'Justification' in the Epistle of James." In *Right with God: Justification in the Bible and the World*, edited by D. A. Carson, 146–62. Grand Rapids: Baker, 1992.

George, Timothy. "'A Right Strawy Epistle': Reformation Perspectives on James." *The Southern Baptist Journal of Theology* 4, no. 3 (Fall 2000): 20–31.

Hartin, P. J. *James and the Q Sayings of Jesus*. Journal for the Study of the New Testament, Supplement Series 47. Sheffield: JSOT, 1991.

Howard, Tracy L. "Suffering in James 1:2–12." *Criswell Theological Review* 1, no. 1 (Fall 1986): 71–84.

Johnson, Luke Timothy. *The Letter of James*. The Anchor Bible. New York: Doubleday, 1995.

_____. "The Use of Leviticus 19 in the Letter of James." *Journal of Biblical Literature* 101, no. 3 (1982): 391–401.

Kamell, Mariam. "The Economics of Humility: The Rich and the Humble in James." In *Economic Dimensions of Early Christianity*, edited by Bruce Longenecker and Kelly Leibengood, 157–75. Grand Rapids: Eerdmans, 2009.

Laato, Tim. "Justification according to James: A Comparison with Paul." *Trinity Journal* 18 (1997): 43–84.

Mahony, John W. "The Origin of Jacobean Thought." PhD diss., Mid-America Baptist Theological Seminary, 1982.

Marshall, I. H. *New Testament Theology: Many Witnesses, One Gospel*. Downers Grove, IL: InterVarsity Press, 2004.

Martin, Ralph P. *James*. Word Biblical Commentary. Waco, TX: Word, 1988.

McCartney, Dan G. "Suffering and the Apostles." In *Suffering and the Goodness of God*, edited by Christopher W. Morgan and Robert A. Peterson, 95–116. Theology in Community. Wheaton, IL: Crossway, 2008.

_____. "The Wisdom of James the Just." *The Southern Baptist Journal of Theology* 4, no. 3 (Fall 2000): 52–64.

Moo, Douglas J. *The Letter of James*. Pillar New Testament Commentary. Grand Rapids: Eerdmans, 2000.

Morgan, Christopher W., and B. Dale Ellenburg. *James: Wisdom for the Community*. Fearn, UK: Christian Focus Publications, 2008.

Motyer, J. A. *The Message of James*. The Bible Speaks Today. Downers Grove: InterVarsity Press, 1985.

Penner, Todd C. *The Epistle of James and Eschatology: Rereading an Ancient Christian Letter*. Journal for the Study of the New Testament, Supplement Series 121. Sheffield: Sheffield Academic Press, 1996.

Richardson, Kurt A. *James*. New American Commentary. Nashville: Broadman and Holman, 1997.

Schreiner, Thomas R. *New Testament Theology: Magnifying God in Christ*. Grand Rapids: Baker, 2008.

Sloan, Robert B. "The Christology of James." *Criswell Theological Review* 1, no. 1 (Fall 1986): 3–30.

Stein, Robert H. "'Saved by Faith [Alone]' in Paul versus 'Not Saved by Faith Alone' in James." *The Southern Baptist Journal of Theology* 4, no. 3 (Fall 2000): 4–19.

Taylor, Mark E. "Recent Scholarship on the Structure of James." *Currents in Biblical Research* 3 (2004): 86–115.

Taylor, Mark E., and George H. Guthrie. "The Structure of James." *Catholic Biblical Quarterly* 68 (2006): 681–705.

Tidball, Derek. *Wisdom from Heaven: The Message of the Letter of James for Today*. Fearn, UK: Christian Focus, 2003.

Wall, Robert W. *Community of the Wise: The Letter of James*. New Testament in Context. Valley Forge, PA: Trinity Press International, 1997.

_____. "James, Letter of." In *Dictionary of Later New Testament and Its Developments*, edited by Ralph P. Martin and Peter H. Davids. Downers Grove, IL: InterVarsity Press, 1997.

Witherington, Ben, III. *Letters and Homilies for Jewish Christians: A Socio-Rhetorical Commentary on Hebrews, James and Jude.* Downers Grove, IL: InterVarsity Press, 2007.

Index of Scripture

204

4:5—151
5:9–10—139
8–9—3n5
12:20—107

Galatians
1—5, 163
1:18–19—3
2:1–6—4
2:9—3
2:9–10—3
2:12—4
3:10—88
5:1–14—121n14
5:6—134
5:13—130
5:16–25—139n25
5:22–23—156
5:22–24—53
6:1–10—113

Ephesians
1:3–14—143
1:13—116–17,
   143
2:1–10—117
2:4–7—143
2:8–10—135, 143
2:10—143
4:11—99
4:26—96–97
4:29–5:4—110
5:24–25—104

Philippians
1:10—153
2:1–11—105
2:3—54
2:6–11—151
2:19—92, 109
2:24—92, 109

Colossians
1:5—116

1 Thessalonians
3:13—152

2 Thessalonians
1:5–11—71n5

2 Timothy
2:9—116
2:15—116
3:12—67
4:2—116

Titus
1:5–9—163

Hebrews
4:12–13—118
6:3—92, 109
11—75
11:6—51
11:31—141

James—15
1—29, 137, 182
1:1—1, 9–10, 14–15, 19, 21–22,
   146, 150, 155, 163, 166
1:1–2—20
1:1–12—43
1:1–18—171
1:1–21—21
1:2—18, 20, 32, 34, 65–70, 161, 174
1:2–3—41, 68
1:2–4—16, 21–22, 47,
   55, 69, 160, 182
1:2–5—149
1:2–8—33–34, 148, 165, 167, 172
1:2–11—22, 42, 68, 72, 112
1:2–12—65–67, 71

209

1:2–18—21
1:2–27—21–22
1:3—70, 133, 174
1:3–4—19, 70, 76
1:4—33–34, 41, 48, 68, 71, 120, 134
1:4–5—19
1:5—18, 33–34, 48–50, 146, 148–49, 156
1:5–6—19
1:5–8—21–22, 47–48, 50, 56–57, 68, 104, 156, 158, 171, 181
1:5–11—43
1:6—19–20, 28, 34, 50, 133
1:6–8—49
1:7—51
1:8—33–34, 50–51, 53, 57, 158, 176
1:9—18, 73, 80
1:9–10—34
1:9–11—16–17, 21–22, 68, 71–72, 74, 78, 80–81, 94, 106, 109, 149, 156, 158, 164–65, 182
1:9–12—66, 71
1:10—80–81, 158
1:10–11—19–20, 25n, 28–29, 81
1:11—18, 29, 81
1:12—22, 34, 61, 68–69, 71–72, 148–49, 159, 165, 167, 182–83
1:12–14—19
1:12–15—167
1:12–18—21, 172
1:13—18, 146, 173
1:13–15—14, 22, 33–34, 72, 157–58, 165, 174, 182
1:13–17—148
1:13–18—55, 117, 149, 157, 159, 180
1:13–27—22
1:14–15—19, 171
1:15—20, 158
1:15–18—167, 181
1:16—161, 174
1:16–17—149
1:16–18—29, 122, 148, 182
1:16–19a—22
1:17—11, 32–34, 120, 146–47, 173
1:18—29, 34, 61, 96, 115–17, 123, 140, 143, 147, 149, 156, 162, 165, 171, 189
1:18–19a—171
1:18–21—58
1:18–25—116, 123
1:19—21, 96, 123
1:19–20—19
1:19–21—21, 43, 95–96, 182
1:19–25—116, 118–19, 167
1:19–27—161, 173
1:19b–21—22
1:19b–25—171
1:20—33–34, 148, 158
1:21—34, 96–97, 115–16, 121, 123, 158, 165
1:22—60, 115, 174
1:22–25—16, 21–22, 27, 33–34, 41, 55, 96, 116, 122–23, 158, 182
1:22–27—27, 43–44, 56, 58, 60, 107
1:22–2:26—21
1:23—19–20, 60, 115, 118, 122
1:24—18, 20
1:25—11, 32, 34–35, 60–61, 115–16, 118, 120–21, 124, 132, 134, 159, 165
1:25–27—149
1:26—82, 95, 97, 100, 158, 171
1:26–27—16, 21–22, 33, 35,

213

Index of Subjects and Names